LOST YOUR BOUNCE ?

COMPOSTING LIFE'S TROUBLES INTO *RESILIENCE*

Jenn Weidman

Copyright © 2023 by Jenn Weidman

All rights reserved.

ISBN 979-8-218-30447-8

Book illustrations and cover design by Kanthicha Mongkornfah

Contents

Preface 7
Chapter 1: On Composting Your Life 13

Chapter 2: Having Some Waste is Normal - 21
It's What You Do With it That's Important
   What It's Not 22
   What It Is 23
   How 24
   Perspective 25
   It's Okay To Have Waste, Compost Relies On It 26
   It's Okay To Get Help 29
   Some Preconditions 30
   Boundaries & Giving Without Refueling 31
   Aloneness & Support 36
   Will & Resources 34
   Building the Path 36

Chapter 3: Setting Up Your Compost System 39
   Design Your Life 39

Chapter 4: Gathering & Separating Your Compostable 43
Material
   Intention, Quality, & Quantity 45

Chapter 5: Add Your Starter 49
   Finding the Spark 50

Chapter 6: Add Your Compostable Material & Keep It Balanced	55
The Resilience Muscle	56
Resilience Practice	59
Reflection	62
Creativity	67
Nature	72
Movement	77
Connection	82
Community	88
Chapter 7: Stir Periodically & Monitor Dampness	93
The Only Constant is Change	95
Grounding	103
Limit Yourself	105
Build Your Path Well	109
Beginning Again … And Again	111
Chapter 8: Curing: Fermentation Takes Time & Space	113
Baby Steps	117
Rest & Wasting Time	118
Epilogue: Grow Your Garden	123
How to Start	123
Some resources that influenced my thinking	129
Acknowledgments	131
About the Author	133

To those who helped me find my bounce again

Preface

"Write hard and clear about what hurts."
- Ernest Hemingway

I wrote this book because when I needed one like it, I couldn't find any. At the time, I had a job I loved that challenged and fulfilled me. I was happy with my life and things were going well. It was definitely not my first time at the rodeo in dealing with difficult, stressful, and challenging work experiences. I was succeeding in my job and had almost completely gotten past the personal aftermath of a year of psychological harassment at a previous job.

The first time it took me the entire work day to write a three sentence email, I knew there was a problem. That email, like many that came after, loomed over me like an unconquerable mountain that I simply couldn't climb. When it was time for me to go home that day, fear and panic descended and spurred me to write the three sentences and send the email.

The same thing happened the next day, and on even more days after that. I couldn't do my work properly except out of fear that someone would discover my incapacity. And working out of fear is definitely not a good place to be. At times the fear wasn't even enough. While it sat with me always, it began to lose its potency to make me move.

There were other symptoms too. I had no energy. No initiative. I felt dead inside. My inner creative spark was completely and utterly gone. I became a hermit outside of work commitments. And I could barely find the energy to even do the dishes at home, much less do anything else. I was forever exhausted and unmotivated. I kept up appearances at my job well enough, but I knew I couldn't go on that way forever, and that someday it would become clear that I had completely lost the fire necessary to succeed.

What was wrong with me? I started wondering if this was what they called burnout. I'd heard about it, but didn't have a clear idea of what it looked like. So I did what we all do these days and turned to Google. What I found wasn't very encouraging and was only minimally helpful. Websites would describe the tiredness and fatigue and apathy, but they didn't go into detail, which left me wondering if things like my email paralysis were also part of burnout or if there was something else going on.

On top of that, all the websites said the same thing about what to do once you discover you are burned out. Unanimously, the answer was quit your job. And that didn't work for me. For various reasons, quitting my job was not really an option at the time. And the effort of pursuing a new job was completely beyond me.

As I thought about it more, I realized that a few of my friends were also burned out, and it was through conversations with them that I was able to confirm that all the strange things I was experiencing were symptoms of burnout. I also saw that quitting their jobs was not really an option for my friends either.

Sometime around then something clicked inside of me. My very being rejected the assumption that the only way to get over burnout was to leave the job that burned you out in the first place. Plus, I didn't quite believe that simply changing jobs would instantly fix everything I was now struggling with. Wouldn't I just carry this struggle into whatever new position I undertook? There had to be more to it and there had to be another way. It had to be possible. Because if not, then there was no hope left for me. And I just couldn't face an indefinitely long future living as a husk of a human.

My real journey began with this realization. I had to find a way out of my burnout while still working in my same job.

Then my situation became compounded when, as I was just beginning to glimpse the possibility of healing, my dad was diagnosed with end stage lung cancer and passed away six months to the day after his diagnosis. I was fortunate to be able to help take care of him and my family for most of those six months, and I will never regret that time. As the difficulty of it and the grief that followed descended, it amplified my burnout, dwarfing all my efforts to heal. Struggles in life don't happen in isolation.

This book, then, is about my journey of healing in pursuit of resilience. I don't write "journey back" because I have learned that you can never go back. There is no going back. There is only wandering the abyss or going forward. Within these pages are some things I've learned, and am still learning, on that journey.

What I know now, is there is much more to learn. This book is in no way a definitive word on resilience. It is, thankfully, one of many. And it is just a starting place.

So, since I've already mentioned the abyss, let's start with a poem by a friend of mine, Di Bretherton, written during a resilience retreat I co-facilitated in 2016:

Silver sliver slide
To the unknown
Face fear, hold the thread
Walk strongly, reach further
Follow the thread
But don't be afraid to let go
Let go
The abyss is a trampoline

Chapter 1
On Composting Your Life

*"Whatever you're meant to do, do it now.
The conditions are always impossible."*
- Doris Lessing

"It'll smell! There'll be bugs! We'll be living with a pile of trash! Don't you dare think about getting worms!" The protests and worries of my family were loud and immediate. I'd just announced that I was going to start composting.

For many people, composting is a quite normal, everyday experience, so let me help you visualize why my family was worried. I live in an apartment in downtown Bangkok, Thailand. My plan was to compost our household kitchen scraps and other appropriate waste on a small balcony. In the middle of the city. In the tropics. What could possibly go wrong?

I'm a farmer and gardener at heart and was becoming increasingly frustrated with the seeming limitations small apartment balconies offer in this regard. Beyond the limited space for growing things, I kept asking myself one question. Why should composting be only for those living in more rural or suburban areas with wider, open spaces? There must be a way for us urban dwellers to get in on the action too.

So I did what I usually do in these situations. I went about learning from others and then putting together various techniques to fit my specific context. And that's how, several days later, I had a plan. I rather think my household was secretly hoping the whole thing would be a dismal failure and that I'd soon give up on this crazy idea. Perhaps to my family's chagrin, my plan worked. Plus, it didn't involve worms as I gave up on the vermicompost approach after a friend of mine told me his challenges in keeping worms alive in Bangkok's stifling heat and roasting sun.

My original plan was simple and effective. First, start with some smaller buckets easily procured from my local stuff mart type store. Second, layer some dry matter in the bottom of the bucket, torn up cardboard egg cartons were my favorite, and dump in a bit of dirt to get things started. Third, get my family to help separate green and brown material for composting, a more challenging task than I might have anticipated - green being the fresh, wet stuff like kitchen scraps and brown being the dry stuff like tissues and paper. Fourth, layer the compost material in the bucket as it comes, making sure to get the green and brown mix correct at about one third green to two thirds brown. Fifth, cover the bucket with an old t-shirt so the compost will be nicely aerated and secure it with elastic or something you can tie and untie easily. Sixth, let the waste do its thing, stirring it weekly. Seventh, I enjoyed my fresh compost, using it for balcony plants and eventually giving it away to my friends when I had too much for my limited balcony space.

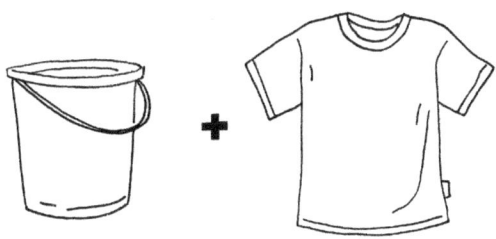

The plan was solid and before long one bucket became two became four became six. The buckets weren't very big and it takes time for matter to decompose so I needed to have several buckets on the go at the same time. But it worked. Every weekend I would stir the buckets, rotating them on the balcony in order to keep track of which was further along in the process than the others. I began to notice that if I was paying attention to what I was doing and how I was layering the waste into the bucket, it came out nicely balanced and decomposed quickly. I could put my hand on the side of the bucket and feel the heat being created by decomposition. Yet, at other times when I was rushed or not really intentional about how I was layering the material, I sometimes ended up with a bucket full of wet stinky slop and needed to add quite a lot of brown matter in order to rescue it. Intention and attention were key to the entire process.

I've been composting for a few years now and have tried several different approaches, learning much along the way. In case you're wondering, my current compost setup is a tier of ceramic pots from PakDone, a local sustainability organization, and I couldn't be happier.

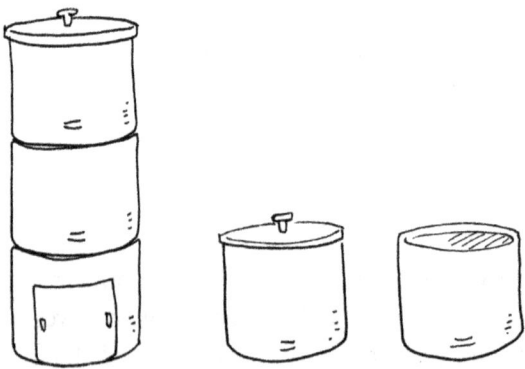

There's something that really excites me about the composting process - garbage from my life sits in a container on my balcony churning itself into rich soil that will nourish my garden of herbs and other plants and, therefore, my body and soul.

Gradually, as I delved deeper into the composting process, a metaphor came. I often seem to have ongoing conversations with friends and colleagues about how we're nurturing our personal and professional projects and our lives. Do we try to take the fast, flash in the pan approach or do we do it the slow, hard way, gradually tilling the soil and nourishing seeds into saplings, into trees, into a forest? And if we're tending our soil and our trees, where is our compost? Are we able to take the garbage in, of, and from our lives and allow it to transform into the rich soil that nourishes our dreams? Or do we attempt to farm in arid land next to a growing mound of trash without ever connecting the two or tapping their hidden potential?

And how, exactly, do we achieve this transformation? What are the thought processes and practices that allow us to churn the garbage of our lives into something nourishing? What do we need to say and do internally to keep churning our garbage into nourishment?

When I talk to people about composting, there are usually some chuckles, a small bit of interest, and a whole lot of people who think I'm crazy. When I start explaining how I've managed to achieve odorless, clean compost on an urban balcony, most people's eyes glaze over and I watch as they look for an exit -

either from the conversation or the room.

When I talk to people about my life compost, that is, the garbage in my life that has transformed into rich lessons, there are still a lot of people who think I'm crazy, but for a different reason. And most people still look for a quick exit. Many people would easily ask me for advice, based on my experience, with difficult management dilemmas, but they would never seek advice from my experiences of workplace harassment, bullying, and toxic atmospheres. They wouldn't dare to even ask if I have personal experience of any sort with those topics, which still seem taboo.

Years ago I was psychologically harassed in the workplace. It lasted a year, during which it took a serious toll on me as I experienced all the personal impacts alongside the usual excuses from those in power. Eventually it ended, and I started working to move on. Now, years later, I'm sometimes a bit surprised at how often lessons from that time in my life come to bear on my present. It seems that bucket of compost is now growing some good trees in the forest that is my life.

Yet, when I recently mentioned my harassment experience in the context of a related discussion and used it to illustrate a few relevant points, the reaction to my admission of harassment was, as usual, notable. There is always a bit of uncomfortable startled surprise that I would discuss this kind of experience, as if I broached a taboo subject. Yet, why wouldn't I? These are serious issues in our workplaces and nothing is learned or gained by keeping them secret, not to mention the incongruity of intent between organizations saying "we want to have a discussion about harassment" and "but please don't share". In my case, the icky, smelly bits have decomposed and what I'm left with is rich, earthy soil to use for whatever comes next. It is part of who I am and how I approach things.

I want to live in a world where we can more freely talk about all our garbage and compost, noting the lessons along the way and building on them as we continue to walk on. And I want to live in a world where we all compost - both physically and metaphorically.

Chapter 2
Having Some Waste is Normal - It's What You Do With It That's Important

*"Caring for myself is not self-indulgence,
it is self-preservation."*
- Audre Lorde

By now you're probably wondering if this is a book about resilience or composting. In truth, it's both. Because they're inextricably intertwined. The coming chapters are organized around the steps to composting and resilience, both physically and metaphorically, which brings us to a central question I mull over regularly: What is resilience?

What It's Not

When I ask people what they think of when they hear the word resilience, the most common words that surface are bouncing back, pushing through, grit, or recovering. It turns out, though, that none of these words quite get there alone.

The idea of resilience being bouncing back from something seemed to make sense to me, until I found myself in the midst of some seriously adverse events in my own life. As I began to consider what moving through to the other side of this experience would mean, I realized with certainty that I would never be the same. The adverse events had changed me irrevocably. There was no going back. There was only moving forward.

People also talk about how to push through in difficult times. For me, this always seems to connote just gritting your teeth and keeping on, regardless of what you're suffering along the way. While I agree that fortitude and grit have a big role to play in resilience, I've seen many lives damaged by a "just suck it up" attitude. Yes, sometimes we need to push. Yet consistent admonishments to suck it up as a complete strategy for life rather than dealing with the sources of the ongoing struggle ultimately help only to further demoralize us. My journey with grief and burnout was not served by just sucking it up. It was only through embracing the pain that movement happened. There was no amount of sucking it up or grinning and bearing it that could have helped me out of my burnout. In fact, those things only helped to dig me in deeper.

Resilience is also not numbness. You feel everything, process it, and move forward in your own time. If you find yourself emotionally unaffected by adverse and upsetting events in your life, what you are probably experiencing is dissociation, not resilience.

I used to relate to the concept that resilience is not in how you bounce back, it is in how you recover. Yet according to the Oxford Dictionary, to recover means to "return to a normal state of health, mind, or strength" or to "find or regain possession of (something stolen or lost)". In this sense, recovery could mean regaining a healthy state of mind or your agency to act. This evokes a sense of returning rather than forward movement and relies on the assumption that you already had a healthy state of mind before the adversity happened in your life. It has the idea of being back to normal, yet normal has forever shifted.

What It Is

Resilience, for me, is in how you keep going and move forward. When adversity strikes, how do you, first, find the energy to keep going, and, second, move forward through it to come out on the other side? Yes, there are certainly elements of bouncing, perhaps forward rather than back, pushing through, as a tool rather than a strategy, and recovering a healthy state of mind and body. Yet individually these things are not enough to fully describe the experience and what I hope to build for myself and encourage in others. What I'm really after is the ability to move forward regardless of difficulty, struggle, or adverse events. I want to be able to employ bouncing, pushing, and recovering as tools along the way on a continual journey forward. I want to avoid being completely derailed or losing all momentum. Even if the forward movement is the tiniest of crawls, it's still something. And slowly, slowly many small some-things become larger and significant and the journey continues. As the line goes, "I may have lost my step, but I never lost my way."

For me, resilience is the ability to sustain work in difficult situations or with difficult issues, and move through adversity in your life with greater wellbeing. It's maintaining the spark, stoking, and feeding the flames of your inner creativity, energy, and force for efficacy and innovation.

Adam Grant, the well-known organizational psychologist and author, has written, "Resilience is not a race to bounce back from hardship. It's a commitment to keep going in the face of hardship."

How

So how do we do it?

This book will explore paths to resilience based on my own experience with burnout and grief, conversations with others about their journeys, and my resilience work with individuals and groups. Note that my journey is one among many, and it's in no way perfect or even a shining example. It's one person's experience in pursuing resilience, and because this pursuit is individual, what worked for me may not work for others. Yet perhaps there are lessons we can learn from our many journeys through difficulty with resilience.

If you picked up this book hoping for answers and a twelve step plan, let's take a moment to manage expectations. The answers to resilience lie inside each of us and are specific to each of us. That means, you have to find the answers yourself. What this book will do is help you start asking the questions. Sorry, no quick fix here. So are you ready for the journey?

Perspective

Where am I coming from on all of this? It starts with this statement: resilience practice is not indulgence, it is imperative.

In his book *Let Your Life Speak*, Parker Palmer writes, "Self-care is never a selfish act - it is simply good stewardship of the only gift I have; the gift I was put on Earth to offer others. Anytime we can listen to our true self, and give it the care it requires, we do so not only for ourselves but for the many lives we touch." Taking care of myself first is the best thing I can do for everything and everyone I care about.

I didn't always have this perspective. I grew up working hard with the idea of hustle as the foundation for all things. I grew up inculcated in the age-old approach of working hard until you retire and then enjoying life. Yes, you could enjoy some things along the way, but mostly you were to be preparing for the future and sacrificing much of the now. The focus was on those golden retirement years when you would be able to do all the things you always wanted.

My dad passed away at the age of 59, so it seems we're not automatically guaranteed those golden years after all.

Zach Galifianakis has said, "Destroy the idea that you have to be constantly working or grinding in order to be successful. Embrace the concept that rest, recovery, and reflection are essential parts of the progress towards a successful and happy life." We need this balance.

I want to actively live my life with presence and intention each day. I don't want to find myself in my retirement years, if I'm lucky, battered and bruised and limping along, trying to get ready for a life of excitement to come. If life is in the living, then I'm not waiting.

It's Okay To Have Waste, Compost Relies On It

Since in many of our cultures and settings talking about the garbage of our lives is taboo, we need to remind ourselves that it's okay to have waste. It's okay to have troubles and struggles. You can't make a smoothie without throwing away some fruit peels. Avoidance of inner struggle is not the goal. The goal is to know how to deal with the garbage we go through in life in a productive way, composting it, and moving forward, cultivating a life even more lush.

Often our troubles and struggles take the form of burnout and depression. Many symptoms seem to overlap, and at the same time, they are not the same thing.

The World Health Organization defines depression this way:

> Depression is a common mental disorder, characterized by persistent sadness and a loss of interest in activities that you normally enjoy, accompanied by an inability to carry out daily activities, for at least two weeks.
>
> In addition, people with depression normally have several of the following: a loss of energy; a change in appetite; sleeping more or less; anxiety; reduced concentration; indecisiveness; restlessness; feelings of worthlessness, guilt, or hopelessness; and thoughts of self-harm or suicide.
>
> Depression is treatable, with talking therapies or antidepressant medication or a combination of these.

In the 11th Revision of the International Classification of Diseases, the World Health Organization defines burnout as an occupational syndrome as follows:

> Burn out is a syndrome conceptualized as resulting from chronic workplace stress that has not been successfully managed. It is characterized by three dimensions: feelings of energy depletion or exhaustion; increased mental distance from one's job, or feelings of negativism or cynicism related to one's job; and reduced professional efficacy.
>
> Burn out refers specifically to phenomena in the occupational context and should not be applied to describe experiences in other areas of life.

Burnout is a joint activity, a combined effort between, minimally, the individual and their office. That is not in any way to say that it is intentional. I imagine that in most instances of burnout, neither the individual nor their organization set out with burnout as their intention. Mostly, I'd warrant, we don't realize that the ways we are working and living are leading us into burnout until it is too late.

It is a slippery slope. My experience most definitely didn't happen overnight. It was a slow process. So much so, that I was completely unaware it was happening. Like the frog slowly being boiled in a pot of water, I didn't know I was in danger until I was already nearly cooked. At the same time, there's a difference between having a bad day here and there and experiencing this lowness as a chronic affliction. Of slipping into burnout, peacebuilder John Paul Lederach has said, "Little by little I was experiencing a deadening of my soul."

Yes. Been there. Done that. Yikes. I don't recommend it.

Many of the meager attempts to address burnout these days don't quite get there. Organizations and companies simply suggesting their employees "just try yoga" and offering discounted gym memberships is not enough. We need real shifts at the structural, social, and industry levels of how we work and how we think about work and work time. This is why my resilience work involves not only individuals, but also teams and organizations. And it is a topic for another book. This book will focus on the individual level of resilience, never losing sight of the fact that it is not the only aspect to all of this.

It's Okay To Get Help

Every gardener goes to the nursery and seeks advice from experts. It's a normal stop along the way in the gardening journey. It's the same with issues of mental health - it's okay to get help. If you need help, specifically professional help, at some point or points in your life, get it.

Resilience is something we need to live our lives with wellness through all their ups and downs. Resilience practice is an approach to building our resilience. Resilience practice is not a substitute for therapy or other treatment for mental health struggles. If you feel you need professional help, please get it.

Resilience is also not a guarantee against mental health struggles or trauma responses to crisis events. It will help us work through these things and continue to move forward. It is not a 100% guaranteed vaccine against them.

We all struggle at different times throughout our lives. When you need professional help, please get it.

Some Preconditions

If burnout doesn't come quickly and surprisingly out of nowhere, then there must be preconditions or elements that we can identify and recognize as increasing the risk of burnout. As I reflect on it afterwards, some of the elements that went into my own burnout included boundaries, or a lack thereof, giving without refueling, feelings of aloneness, and feeling a lack of support. I was also working in a job that included some heavy content, and in the midst of taking care of others, I wasn't intentional enough about taking care of myself and processing my experiences.

Yet it wasn't until I was already burned out and had become aware of that fact that I began to really see the elements in my work situation that had contributed to my burnout and consider how I might adjust them or at least mitigate their impacts. Before that, I felt the impacts of these issues but did not clearly identify them or know what to do about it.

When I look back on it, the risk indicators for burnout in my job were loud and clear. As I experienced it, work was just work. It had its ups and downs but I didn't recognize anything as warning flags at the time. Now I look at work situations differently, actively seeking to understand dynamics that may lead to burnout so I can proactively address them.

In working with many people in their professional situations and seeing the warning signs from the outside, I regularly consider how we can get a better view of our own work realities from the inside. Can we see the risks and mitigations of burnout in our work life before the water in our pot boils and we're cooked?

The first step to seeing the risk points is to better understand them and how they work.

Boundaries & Giving Without Refueling

My job involved running all aspects of an intensive capacity building program for amazing peacebuilders from around the world for three months at a time, twice a year. During each three-month session, I got to know the participants in the program well. We shared much, both personally and professionally, and therefore both the personal and professional demands on me were high. When I started the job, I gave no thought to the impact this would have on me personally and therefore did not actively consider the idea of boundaries. Besides, I thought, when I did eventually start to think about it, if a significant part of my job was connecting with people, wouldn't boundaries get in the way of that?

Little did I know that in reality it was quite the opposite.

So, without any thought to boundaries, I gave and gave and gave, also never paying attention to how I was refueling myself, if at all. I was looking after the wellbeing of others physically, intellectually, and emotionally, but I was not putting attention into looking after myself.

For the first couple years, all was fine. I was an active person, pursuing hobbies and other interests that unknowingly helped prolong my stamina for the job. But since I was not actively aware of what was happening to me and was not actively processing what I was doing and experiencing, eventually it caught up with me.

I find that awareness and intention around processing and recharging to be seminal. For me, around the time I started my job, I also began learning martial arts. Learning something new, exercise, meditation, and mindfulness are all often part of our journey forward through burnout and in building resilience. And they're all elements I found in my martialarts practice. Perhaps because of that, it took longer for me to feel the effects of burnout than it otherwise would have. What was missing, however, was the awareness and intention.

Essentially, I was accidentally helping myself along. Like recharging a battery that's not properly connected to the charger, I was getting some, but it wasn't deep and full.

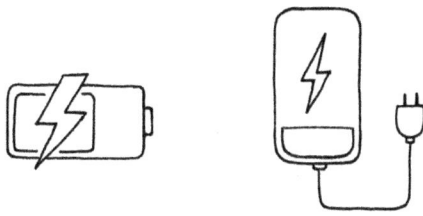

Aloneness & Support

Being the boss can be lonely. For me, I didn't feel much support from my own boss, I had no peers on an equal level in the office, and my colleagues were all my direct reports, meaning while they supported me in work tasks, they could not be confidants. When I began to feel this aloneness and lack of support, as if I was drifting on my own and yet still responsible for absolutely everything, I recognized it, but did not clearly know what to do about it. And then, when it started to get really bad, I was already suffering from the effects of burnout and did not have the energy or impetus to reach out to others for support.

These days, I approach this much differently. I'm still the boss and have no peers in my office, but I proactively find them elsewhere. I create my own community of like minded people with similar or relatable professional situations, and we meet and chat regularly, supporting each other and banishing that feeling of aloneness. Even though we don't do the same sort of work, we still support each other - some problems and experiences are applicable across professions. Also, we don't come to the group always seeking the solution to our problems. Sometimes we come just seeking affirmation and support from others who share similar sorts of stresses and challenges. There's no judgment in this space. We know that no one can succeed professionally on their own. We need support, we need community, and we need it in place and active before things fall apart.

Will & Resources

In his book, *The Infinite Game*, Simon Sinek talks about the juxtaposition of running a business as if we're playing a finite or infinite game. A finite game has all the trappings of your favorite sport. There are rules, there are easily identified players, and there's a goal of winning and a clear definition of how that can happen.

Infinite games, on the other hand, have no known end and no established rules. Instead, they function within a broadly defined frame, allowing players to play as they wish, regardless of whether their actions are aligned with established conventions or not. Players are in full control of how they play the infinite game at every moment, and have full freedom to make adjustments any time they want. Since infinite games have no end, they are impossible to win. The goal, instead, is to keep playing.

While Sinek's book is aimed at business leaders, I see many parallels for how we design and live our lives. If we understand that the goal of the game of life, if you will, is to keep playing rather than win at some arbitrarily determined finish line that will forever shift ahead of us, it relieves us from the pressure to succeed in more conventional ways and frees us to think about what a life well lived might look like for us.

In an infinite game, players stop playing when they run out of will or resources. In life, resources can be physical, mental, spiritual, and more. It sounds like resilience. In the depths of my burnout, I had run out of resources. While I still had a will to live on most days, I did not have the energy, mental, or inspirational resources to continue in the game. Now I try to look after both my will and my resources more carefully.

What exactly are your resources in life? I'm not talking about your money or your things. Your resources are your very self: your energy, your mental state, your physical health, and more. How can we keep our resources replenished?

Your will to live is intertwined with hope and a vision for the future. In her book, *The Lightmaker's Manifesto*, Karen Walrond writes, "I will never apologize for embracing joy and beauty - even when the world is falling apart - because joy and beauty are my fuel for activism."

What is the fuel for your life? Where does your hope and vision for the future lie? How can you hold on to this even when the world is falling apart?

Building the Path

I often think of my burnout, grief, and other difficult times as a deep hole I fell into. As an old Billy Sprague song describes it:

> I was down in the valley of the shadow of death
> Where the passion for life drained like blood from my chest
> And it took more than my will just to take a step
> And the comfort of hope was gone
>
> In a silence so black that I wished for the Blues
> Every desperate prayer seemed like heaven refused
> And some days I found faith in just tying my shoes
> And it was all I could do to press on

The walls of that hole are slippery, and it is hard to climb out. When you're at the bottom of the hole, it seems much easier to give up, give in, and stay there. Yet that's not a way to live.

To climb out, you have to build a path and walk it bit by bit, one step at a time. And it's not linear. You may move forward or backward or sideways. That's ok, because it's a journey with no pre-existing paths. As Antonio Machado has said, "Travelers, there is no path, paths are made by walking."

So how do you begin the journey out and forward? Once I had identified my burnout, that was my next question. Not only was "quit your job" not an option, I innately knew that simply leaving my job would not heal me. The surrounds of the deep hole I was in might change, but I'd still be there, at the bottom of the hole. Burnout is not the best place from which to start a new job, if I could even muster enough energy to find one.

Where did that leave me? How do you start walking a path up slippery walls out of a deep hole?

If you've ever tried to scale a smooth and slippery slope, you'll quickly realize that walking directly upwards doesn't work. It is too steep and too slippery and you will find yourself falling backwards quickly. If you do manage to make some progress, it will be because you temporarily found a foothold or handhold to help support you, or that you charged with such speed and force that you managed to make some progress. Still, if we're talking about a wall of significant height, at some point you will need to pause to regroup before you launch your next push upwards. And in this pause, you may find your foothold sliding back down.

What I realized is that there is no super fast, direct way out. More like a road engineer cutting roads through the mountains, you must cut a path into the walls around you. Building this path allows you to pause, to regroup, and to make easier progress forward after you've inevitably stumbled backwards. It seems to be harder work than simply trying to charge straight up the wall, but it is the only way out. There are no shortcuts.

When I started composting, I realized something else. While you're building your path, you're also composting your life garbage into rich soil you can stand on and grow things in, thus making your path easier.

Chapter 3
Setting Up Your Compost System

"People do not decide their futures, they decide their habits and their habits decide their futures."
- F. M. Alexander

Design Your Life

In his book *Essentialism: The Disciplined Pursuit of Less*, Greg McKeown talks about "living by design, not by default", that "if you don't prioritize your life, someone else will", and the "invincible power of choice".

McKeown describes choice not as something we have, but rather something we do. When viewed in this way, we can differentiate between our options and our active choice.

While we often may not have control over some of our options, we can always control what we choose.

Our options can come and go and even be taken away from us. But our ability to make choices is forever ours alone. It cannot be taken away, it can only be forgotten. Slowly, slowly we often surrender our choices and allow others to choose for us, gradually teaching ourselves to be helpless. Eventually we forget our free will to the point that our lives are solely the result of other people's choices for us alongside the long term impacts of choices we once made when we still knew how. We have completely given the power and permission of our life choices to others.

Choice is an action. And if we don't make our own choices, someone else will make them for us. Sometimes that's ok. Sometimes it's fine to let someone else decide what's for dinner, how to complete the household errands today, or where we're going on vacation. In terms of our resilience and the balance of our lives, however, those choices should sit squarely with us.

We need to be active and proactive about how we allocate our time. We need to think in terms of designing our lives in such a way as to promote our own resilience and that of those around us. We need to set our own priorities to help us balance our lives and all the many responsibilities we juggle within them. We need to create the best compost system that works for us. If your journey is anything like mine, this means it will take some experimentation to find what works best.

We all have constraints in our lives. An acquaintance once challenged me by saying that we all make choices. We had been talking about the privilege he had in leaving his home and work for months on end to pursue his passions and the conversation had come around to the perspective that not everyone has that sort of freedom in their life. His challenge, then, was that everyone can do anything, it's about our choices. We can choose to walk away from our responsibilities and families and let them sink or swim on their own while we pursue something else. We have that choice.

For me, things fall somewhere in the middle. There are constraints in my life that exist because of things I can't control - like where I was born, etc. There are also constraints in my life that I choose that I will never un-choose - like the family responsibilities I have. Within this framework, there are many choices, both large and small, that I make freely on both short term and long term trajectories, and there are those I let others make for me.

My compost system must somehow fit within my constraints. I have limited small balcony space with certain sun exposure and weather patterns I cannot change. I gave up on the idea of vermicompost, for example, when I realized that the sun exposure on my balconies might just cook the poor worms in their home. Since baked worms wasn't my goal, I chose something else.

I can spend endless time dreaming of a nice corner in a plot of land I don't have in which I could construct what many would see as a "proper compost setup", but that is not my reality. At the moment, the option of that kind of compost system is not available to me. Yet the choice to set up a compost system is very much mine. I just need to choose the system that will work best for me, whether it's a series of buckets, a tumbler that somehow fits in my limited space, or a ceramic tower of decomposition.

If, as French ballerina and choreographer Marie-Agnes Gillor says, "Discipline is the cornerstone of freedom, not the opposite", then perhaps some constraint provides the right conditions for creativity. We all have a frame within which we live our lives. Parts of that frame are given to us and others we choose, not to be un-chosen. It is up to us, then, to get creative within that frame and actively design our lives, and our compost systems. What do you want your life to look like? What really are your priorities? How can you design your life to reflect that?

Chapter 4
Gathering & Separating Your Compostable Material

*"Stop measuring days by degree of productivity
and start experiencing them by degree of presence."
- Alan Watts*

Now that you've got your compost system set up and ready to go, it's time to gather and separate your compostable material. For good compost, you'll need both green and brown material. In general, bigger pieces take longer to compost, which is something to consider if you have limited space like I do. I always cut kitchen waste, for example, into smaller chunks for faster composting results. Also, some items just take longer than others to fully break down.

After one particularly fruitful mango season, I ended up with a lot of mango peels and pits. While the peels broke down quickly, I kept moving the pits from bucket to bucket as they took longer than the rest of my material and hadn't finished breaking down even when the other matter around them had. Eventually, I ended up with a bucket full of mango pits in different stages of decomposition. And then I unknowingly did the best thing I could have done - I went away for a month or two. When I came back, I found the most beautiful bucket of dirt. Mango pits take a long time to fully compost, but they make great dirt if you are willing to wait.

At the same time, some things just never seem to break down, while others don't actually need to be composted. Lychee seeds, for example, will stay in your compost bin interminably. I find it better to use them as filler in the bottom of my pots for good drainage. If you just made some fresh Roselle juice by boiling some fresh Roselle flowers until they've given up their deep ruby red juice, there's no need to compost the remaining flower solids. I like to pop them into a blender with other fruit and make a smoothie instead. Not everything we go through in life needs a long and involved time to process. Sometimes we can just make a smoothie and move forward. Other things will be with us in one way or another forever, so we'd better set about finding a way and place in our life for them to be useful.

Intention, Quality, & Quantity

I have a good friend with a full life and high-powered job. When we hang out, it's usually for finite amounts of time between other commitments. Yet, afterwards, I feel more connected, seen, heard, full, and warm and fuzzy than some times when I've spent whole days with other friends. So what's the difference? I think it is intention.

When my friend and I grab a quick coffee between other commitments, or call each other up with an invitation to our regular noodle shop because we have a spare 45 minutes in our day, we bring a certain intention every time. When we sit down with each other, we consciously put aside the many other things going on in our days, look into each other's eyes, and connect. Sometimes we talk about deep life direction questions, while other times our conversation is lighter. Regardless, we are there to be there. We refuse distraction, focusing only on the other person for that space of time. There's no need to worry - we know the distractions will still be there waiting for us after we've had our coffee. We choose to suspend the seemingly urgent in favor of intentionally engaging in the important.

These regular moments of intentional connection have more impact in our lives than the once in a long time big events. In the constant balance between quantity and quality, it seems quality with intention wins just about every time.

What does this mean for our resilience practice?

First, it means that it is, in fact, a practice. Something we do regularly throughout our lives. There will be no finally achieving it. It should be as natural as brushing our teeth, albeit with more intention if you are like me and use your teeth brushing moments to space out a bit. And we will need to adjust and refine it along the way, rather like changing toothpastes or tooth brush designs, adopting a new brushing motion, or changing the length of time you brush.

Second, it means it can be small things. We don't necessarily need to go on a massive hike every other day, and at the same time you can do that if you want to. Yet mostly it is more about putting together smaller moments throughout your days and weeks and months and years. As John Steinbeck has said, "Just set one day's work in front of the last day's work. That's the way it comes out. And that's the only way it does." All of this encourages me to think about each day as a series of choices I get to make that support my resilience and wellbeing or don't. I don't have to always look at the huge picture. Sometimes it's just this choice right here, right now. While I can see how that could be stressful for some, for me, it's freeing.

If I stay grounded in the power of consistent, intentional baby steps, then this choice I make right now is all I need. I can take each small choice as it comes. It simply becomes about things I can do. I'm not stressing over a need to conquer huge mountains instantly. I'm trying to be present in my life and make intentional decisions throughout my day.

To be clear, I'm not always successful in maintaining this perspective. I feel overwhelmed regularly and I question myself and my path often. Perhaps one of the most ironic oft repeated internal conversations I have with myself has all the trappings of a whiny "are we there yet?!?!" question from a child in the back seat of a car on a long drive to a family vacation destination.

Ultimately, one of the challenges with resilience practice is that there's actually no "there" waiting in the future. It is a lifelong practice we will always be pursuing. There will never be a day when we can say: "Ok great. I've done it. Resilience achieved forever so no need to work on that any more. What's next?" It will always be our small choices every day.

For me, then, these thoughts on intention and consistency mean we can chill, which, in some ways, is part of the point. Resilience practice shouldn't be something to stress about. It also shouldn't be just one more thing to check off on your to do list, although I admit that sometimes it can feel like that.

Chapter 5
Add Your Starter

*"Hope is holding a creative tension between what is
and what could and should be,
each day doing something to narrow the distance
between the two."*
- Parker J. Palmer

With your composting system ready and your compostable waste being separated, we need to think about how to get this whole process of decomposition started. Best practices of composting say that you need to have some sort of starter to begin with in your compost system. Usually this is something like a handful of dirt or a bit of compost from a previous batch. For our human composting of difficulties, this starter is our inner spark.

Finding the Spark

Sitting in the midst of my burnout feeling a complete lack of life and energy started my ongoing contemplation about the spark inherent to all humans. I like to think of it as a little fire burning inside each of us. I usually tend to feel it in my chest, but I think I've also felt it in my brain. Some people call it passion or purpose or spirit or inspiration. I'll refer to it as the fire inside of us, or the spark.

So where does it come from? I think we are all born with it. But, like our bodies, just because we are born with it doesn't mean that we can ignore it or take it for granted - that it doesn't need tending to.

Before my burnout I had never thought about the fire inside. To be honest, I often never even noticed it beyond random feelings of inspiration from time to time that I didn't really understand. I still don't, by the way, but I'm working on it.

Yet, like a physical fire, our inner spark goes through cycles of burning brightly and dying down to embers. And, also like a physical fire, it needs to be fed and maintained regularly.

Keeping a campfire going for an extended period of time takes maintenance. After you've laid the kindling and quick burn material, you light it with a spark from somewhere - a match or lighter or a flint if you're old school. Once you've got it going, you have to actively tend it, pushing logs into better places, adding more as needed, or building it up if it burns down too low. And it needs the right fuel. Add too much light weight kindling and your fire will burn out in a flash. Add too many heavy logs too fast and your fire will suffocate before it really gets going.

In the depths of my burnout, I realized that my fire had completely gone out. Not even a barely glowing ember or spark remained. Nothing. So how was I to restart my fire? A box of matches wasn't going to help me with this. Where could I find the spark to rekindle the fire inside?

Honestly, I had no idea. On top of that, I had no energy or impetus to do anything. Not only did I not know where to look for a spark, I also wasn't really able to go looking at all.

I started wondering how other people overcome adversity. Surely someone else had already found a match. How do they relight and then feed their inner fires to keep going?

I like movies. I like books. I like music. I like a good story. Perhaps, I wondered, if I watch the stories of others, I might learn something. Perhaps I can catch a bit of their spark.

So I decided to watch inspiring, hopeful movies in which people overcame challenges. And, perhaps key to this, I decided to stop double screening and, instead, really watch the movie. I didn't think of it like this at the time, but I had decided to bring intention to this effort - to observe and try to learn from how the characters drew their inspirations and energy to keep going and overcome. I decided the movies had to be hopeful, but of course that did not mean the main characters had to win. I figured this was something I could actually do. I was already well accomplished at collapsing on the couch, so why not use that time to try to get my composting process going and rekindle my inner spark.

Now, I'm not saying this is THE way. As I've said before, everyone's journey with burnout and resilience is different. What worked for me may well not work for you. And that's ok. Find the next step that works for you and start building your path. If you're not sure, just try something you think you can manage. It might work and it might not. But the trying makes the journey and you'll only know how it all fits together once you look back from further down the path. Start by looking for the fire around you. Then pay attention with intention, and see if you can catch some sparks.

At any rate, I started watching movies. Fiction, nonfiction, whatever. As long as they were hopeful with themes of overcoming difficult challenges. So, yes, I watched a lot of sports story movies. Why not? I mean, at that point what did I have to lose, really?

And, believe it or not, it started to work. I would come home from faking it at work, start a movie, and plop myself on the couch for the duration. I would watch closely how the characters managed, what they did, what they said, their facial expressions, how they related to each other, everything. I'd imagine what they were feeling, let the music fill me, appreciate the cinematography, and breathe in that hopeful feeling at the end.

Slowly, slowly, slowly I felt the darkness lifting just a bit and inner light gradually returning. One baby step at a time, I was starting to walk out of the hole I had fallen into. I was starting to compost.

Chapter 6
Add Your Compostable Material & Keep It In Balance

*"Resting is not a waste of time.
It's an investment in wellbeing.
Relaxing is not a sign of laziness. It's a source of energy.
Breaks are not a distraction.
They're a chance to refocus attention.
Play is not a frivolous activity.
It's a path to connection and creativity."
- Adam Grant*

It's time to really get things going now that we've decided to start composting, got our compost system set up, are preparing our compostable material, and have our starter ready. We need to add our compostable material, keeping it in balance between the green and brown matter. And it needs to become a habit. It's easy to forget that the piece of garbage we are holding is compostable. Our human conditioning of simply throwing it on a trash pile and ignoring it can take over quickly if we haven't established our new composting habit well.

The Resilience Muscle

"Let's begin." A room full of about 16 people gaped at the man leading the session. We were there for a body movement session but no one had stretched or limbered up or warmed up in any way. "No, you don't need to stretch." We gaped at him again.

Four hours of constant movement and body weight strength positions later and most of the room was having trouble continuing. We'd had one, short five-minute break for a small gulp of water and a quick visit to the bathroom if the line allowed. And this was day one.

I woke up on the second day painfully stiff. Go figure. Different people have different ideas about stretching before and after physical activity, and I had heard the theory about not doing any stretching at all because of a risk of damaging your muscles if you've stretched them out too much. Personally, I prefer stretching and warming up before physical activity and then doing a deeper stretch after. Jumping right into strenuous physical activity without warming up my body properly never quite works for me.

Plus, there's an age component to this. I realized along the way during that two-day session that I was probably about 10 years older than most of the others in the room, including the leader. It definitely makes a difference.

As I trudged to the venue for day two, every step a strain on my complaining muscles, I encountered others in the session and quickly realized I wasn't the only one suffering. Once we got to the room, some obviously limping with great effort, we all immediately started stretching until the leader called us to begin. The four hours that followed absolutely destroyed what was left of our muscles.

Why? No fitness level was listed as a requirement for the two-day course, and it turns out many in the room were not at that time regularly physically active. Some were just healing from injuries while others had come seeking inspiration for reinvigorating their exercise practices that had fallen out of their regular routines. Those of us who were more physically active were still unprepared as we had not known what to expect and had not warmed up properly. Thus, we were all completely unprepared for eight hours of constant movement with nonstop body weight strength training elements. We weren't ready, and when we called on our muscles to support this difficult, sustained activity they weren't prepared for, they struggled. So when I went to work the next day, I had a very hard time lowering myself onto a chair. You've been there, right?

Some years before this physically punishing experience, as I started to feel encouraged and lighter with the help of my cinematic friends, I began to have just enough energy to think about what my next steps would be on this journey. Certainly simply watching movies wasn't the full answer to my problem. So what was?

I started to think about how I had gotten there in the first place and to look more closely at how I approached my life, my work, and what was possible and not possible. I thought about those things that are life giving to me, that build and recharge my energy, and, conversely, those things that had been sucking my energy dry for so many years. I needed a clearer picture if I was to figure out how to not only fully climb out of this hole, but also stay out in the long term.

It turns out, resilience is a muscle. Like all muscles, you need to train it in order for it to be there for you when you really need it to work well. Burning yourself out and then desperately rushing to a quick vacation or weekend at the beach while frantically wishing it will fix you, and then rushing back home, arriving in a mess of stress and laundry to an inordinately large pile of waiting tasks in your inbox doesn't really work.

Yet that doesn't stop us from hoping it will.

Training our resilience muscle takes the same intention, discipline, thought, and commitment that it takes to train other muscles in our bodies. I soon came to discover that building resilience and making healthy choices for my physical health were intertwined - and that they are both lifelong practices. Just like how we must continue to look after our physical health throughout our lives, we also need to keep working on our resilience in parallel. We need consistent resilience practice. And just as we'll never say, "That's it, I'm fit! No need to exercise ever again," we'll also never be able to say the same about our resilience.

Resilience Practice

> *"A river cuts through rock, not because of its power,*
> *but because of its persistence."*
> *- Jim Watkins*

As we already know, one of the tricks with resilience practice is that it will be different for everyone. There is no prescribed set of steps to building resilience that we can follow. We each need to reflect, explore, experiment, and discover what works for us. That said, there are some ways we can think about all of this to start figuring out what works for us.

Resilience practice is, essentially, how you design and live your life to foster your own resilience. It includes your perspectives, your surroundings, your approaches, and things you do. And, of course, it needs to be a regular thing with some consistency.

I like to think about all of this as a resilience continuum, with self care on one side, resilience practice on the other, and many points in between.

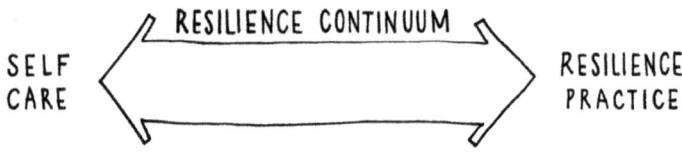

Self care is an often misused word that, in its true meaning, is indeed resilience practice, meaning caring for the self. In most senses these days, however, we see self care used in shallower ways. It might invoke images of manicures, shopping therapy, binge watching Netflix, or going out for a drink. And of course the reality is that these activities may actually be part of your resilience practice. Sometimes what I really need IS actually to watch something engrossing or have a good chat with a friend.

In this way, self care sits on one end of the continuum. This is the emergency room – those things you do when the world is crashing in and you just need to cope. These are the bandages and tourniquets we turn to when we've come home at the end of a particularly hard and stressful day or week at the office, when we are facing our failures, or when our boss has once again overlooked or taken credit for our work. So we turn to something that will make us feel better right now.

On the other end of the continuum is resilience practice. This is prevention and long-term care and treatment – those things you do and practice in the long term that help you reflect, process, and build your personal resilience to sustain you both personally and professionally. This is where you continually stoke the flames of your inner creativity and how you keep your inner fire burning well and long term.

All points along the continuum are important. Just like with our physical health, at various times we need immediate care, diagnostic examinations, good life habits, and long-term practices to continue to sustain our health – both mental and physical. Yes, the details of what works vary for each person and can only be discovered by that individual.

Thus, the path to building our resilience is first a personal journey of exploration inwards.

Reflection

Reflection is both a roadblock and a doorway to everything else. Reflection necessitates an inward journey, which tends to raise some fears. Sitting in silence with myself is uncomfortable. What if I find I don't like myself? There are some things inside me I'd rather ignore. It's much nicer to think of myself as I imagine I am or as I want to be rather than as I actually am right now.

Effective resilience practice must be grounded in knowledge of the self and pursuit of continued learning about one's self. It means we need to confront our inner demons and work through our issues. We need to make peace with who we are right now. Yes, we can seek to change, and we also cannot ignore who we are in the process.

The good news is that we don't have to do all those things all at once. Resilience is a journey taken step by step. We can walk slowly into it. I like to think about reflection in two broad categories: the thinking kind and the not thinking kind.

The thinking kind might include moments when you are actively contemplating something. Perhaps you are writing in your journal at the end of the day, or, in my case, writing your daily haiku. Perhaps you are considering a crucial life question, or unpacking and learning from an experience. You are essentially intentionally musing about something or other.

The not thinking kind might include moments where you are not really doing anything at all - perhaps just bringing stillness to your mind and body. It might also include moments when you are indeed doing something, perhaps something repetitive. Something where your hands are busy and your mind is free to wander. Peacebuilder John Paul Lederach has called this aimless time.

I first began to consciously appreciate the value of aimless time while working pieces of wood into talking sticks with John Paul. We stood in the driveway in front of the open garage of his then house, called Alpenglow, situated in the Colorado mountains near Rollinsville, just above Boulder. Looking out on a spectacular view of the majestic great continental divide, we worked small pieces of wood. We selected

our piece, whittled with knives, and sanded them with sand paper before finally finishing them off with some oil. The process is deeply reflective - an exploration of both the self and the piece of wood, working on both in the process.

One of my colleagues later asked John Paul to work some wood while simultaneously recording himself reflecting out loud on the process. This is what he recorded:

> When I work with wood, I find myself losing track of time. I am lost, and yet totally present. These spaces provide me with the simultaneous experience of remembering and forgetting. My presence in these spaces is aimless. My mind becomes aimless. It wanders and yet is intensively focused. And this becomes a meditative space. Aimless time, I find deeply healing. I have so many challenges in my work that I cannot think my way through. But I can give myself the gift of aimless time, of having no purpose other than what is in my hands at this present moment. I follow my hands, my eyes, my gut, and here is the paradox of aimless time: it is the beginning of creative time, of innovation, of breakthrough.

This perfectly sums up my personal experience with aimless time. In moments when another colleague and I needed to plan something new, something creative that we'd never done before, we did it sitting around outside working wood together. We talked as we worked, with silent moments in between. We took turns noting down our ideas, plans, and decisions. Months later, as the event we were preparing was approaching, we revisited our plans. We were amazed at what we had written together and clearly saw how much better it was than anything we could have done if we had just sat in a room to try to think our way through it. It turns out that aimless time is essential, and that wasting time together is never a waste.

Maybe working wood isn't your thing. That's ok. I've spoken with people who find the same effect when washing dishes, sweeping the floor, running, doing slow movement like tai chi, or doing hand stitching. While I'm slightly envious of those who actually enjoy cleaning their house, I also know that what works for each of us is different and we must find our own way.

So where in all of this does meditation fall? Perhaps it falls into either or neither category, thinking and not thinking, depending on how you practice meditation. I like to keep categories as guidelines to help me think about things, and I don't feel the need to assign them with finality. So I'll leave it there and let you make what you will of how you think about and practice meditation.

One thing that most reflective activities have in common is mindfulness - being present, here and now, with where you are and what you are doing. Not worrying about what's coming next. Not planning our next steps or preparing for what tomorrow holds. Just surrendering to the here and now and letting it be enough.

For me, mindfulness walks alongside intention in resilience

practice. It helps even fleeting moments to be meaningful.

We can see it in John Paul's description of his experience with working wood, and we can experience it in other ways with other activities or non-activities; that state of complete focus, or even being entirely engrossed in something. I have had this experience working wood, even if sometimes it is only for fifteen minutes. I've also lost myself in it for hours on end.

Sometimes I need to be intentional about my mindfulness. If I find I'm stressed, or keyed up, or rushing, and I also find myself making dinner, I'll intentionally make dinner mindfully. To be honest, I now often cook mindfully even when I'm not stressed.

When you put the onions and garlic and other aromatics into the pot or pan to sweat first, my reaction is always to rush the process. Actually, for me it starts even before that with pre-heating the pan and olive oil. "It's fine, it's hot enough, it will heat up more as it cooks. Let's get this going - good food, now, please!" Followed by: "The aromatics are done enough,

let me add the next ingredients now, no need to wait, let's get this moving a bit faster."

In these moments, I try to get intentional about my mindfulness. I flip the script playing out in my head, willfully slowing my body down, breathing deeply, and connecting my senses to the fragrant sizzling happening in the pot. I focus on the quality and depth of the flavors. I think about crafting the dish or meal well. And I am more observant, paying more attention to what's happening to the ingredients in the pot throughout the whole process.

Needless to say that at the end, I have both a better meal and a better mindset to move forward. Plus, it doesn't actually take much more time than rushing through the cooking process. Who knew?

The key consideration to all of this is how and where can we intentionally include reflection and mindfulness in our daily lives. What could that look like for you?

Creativity

The most common response I get when I start talking about creativity is: "Oh, I'm not a creative person." Nonsense. Everyone is creative, it just looks different on each person. First, let's explore a bit about what creativity actually is.

In his 2014 TEDx talk in Sydney, Australia, Linsey Pollak defines creativity as "the putting together of two previously unrelated things, could be objects or ideas, and creating something new." Of course, he says this while making a carrot clarinet live on stage out of a saxophone mouthpiece, a plastic funnel, and, yes, a carrot. I play this five-minute talk often for many audiences. And I always look at their faces when, at the very end, he plays his newly constructed carrot clarinet. They can't help it. Their faces light up in surprise and amazement: "How is THAT sound coming out of a CARROT?!?!" Indeed.

How can we have creative ideas like the carrot clarinet? Where does the creative impulse sit? Remember that fire inside? For me, creativity also sits there. In that spark and flame. It is the reason that when our inner fire goes out, we lose our creativity. It is also the reason that doing creative things can help feed or even re-spark our fire.

So what, exactly, are creative things? Here is where we start to run into trouble as a society. When people tell me, "I'm not a creative person", what they're really saying is: "I don't fit society's definition of creative because I don't/can't do the recognized creative things." In other words, I'm not an artist. And yet I think most of us are artists in our own ways.

Society tends to define creativity in terms of The Arts. My problem, as Chimanande Adiche has said about stereotypes, isn't that this definition is incorrect, it is that it is incomplete. Painting, sculpture, music, dance, pottery, performance, etc. are of course all creative acts. So is writing. I just don't think creativity is limited to these realms.

Once we as a society define creativity in this more narrow perspective, we then seek to value it, and here is where we run into the next bit of trouble.

As children, we are all creative by all definitions. We draw, dance, sing, bang out beats on pots and pans, play imaginary games with imaginary friends, and we are fully committed to our art. Then we go to school, and suddenly our drawing or artwork is placed in a competition with the rest of our classmates and valued as not good enough. Or we try out for the school musical or band and don't get a singing part or a respectable level chair position. Slowly slowly we internalize the idea that creative, artistic acts are worthless and a waste of time unless you are good enough to make a living at it. We should, instead, be seeking to make a living at a 'real' job that will provide what we need and have some measure of stability. We should give up on our artistic dreams.

This is wrong. The point of art isn't to sell it. The point of art IS the art. It is the process of making it. It is stepping back and experiencing it when it is finished. We make art for ourselves. Because we need to. Because we need to express ourselves and create. Because we are all creative.

While an avid home cook and baker, during the Covid-19 pandemic, I did not join the bandwagon and start making sourdough bread - but my friend did. Many weekends would see her messaging me that a loaf was on the way to my house. It was lovely to eat her fresh, homemade sourdough bread and I enjoyed talking about it with her and learning from her experience. And then she moved to another country.

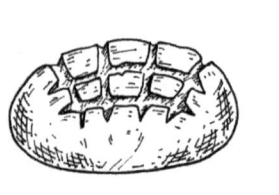 

Before she left, she showed up at my door carrying a bag of supplies and a jar holding her sourdough starter. "This is Kalil. Please take care of him." And so I became a sourdough bread baker.

Some time later, I was in a cooking supply shop casually looking at a bread knife while waiting in line to pay for my other purchases. Two French gentlemen were standing near me and we got to talking about the knife. I wondered if they thought it was any good. They asked what sort of bread I was cutting. I told them sourdough, and, rather proudly I must admit, showed them pictures of my loaves. They seemed impressed and asked, "So you sell this?" I said no. I give it away to friends. They asked again, "So you are selling your bread, right?" No. Just making it for me and I give extra loaves away to my friends. "But surely you are selling this?!" No.

I don't make bread to sell it. And I have a suspicion that if I did monetize my baking it might become more pressured and less enjoyable. I make it for the process, the enjoyment of working with Kalil (yes, he's still alive and well and thriving), of tuning into the dough and its needs throughout the many steps of making the bread, and of course for the delicious results and my friends' reactions as they tuck into a freshly baked loaf. Food, after all, is for sharing.

Society and how we understand the idea of hustle would try to guilt me into monetizing my bread baking. Personally, I choose to rebel and keep it small, personal, and meaningful to me and my friends. And it's enough. The meaning isn't in the money, it's in the doing and, in this case, in the sharing and eating.

Creativity looks different on different people. The psychometric analysis system Emergenetics notes different ways that different people are creative, including convening people, designing a process, creating order out of chaos, painting pictures, and more. What about chefs? What about computer programmers? What about people who solve a lot of problems or design systems or organize things well? What about the hobby gardener, or the person who makes the most amazing spreadsheets? What about all of us in big and small corners of our lives? We are all creative.

Flexing our creativity is extremely good for our resilience. I often encourage people to do those things they stopped doing when they were taught that it was a waste of time if they couldn't monetize it. I've done creative and artistic activities with groups of high powered international business executives, long time government officials, and others. The impact is always significant.

So what are your creative outlets? Of course, only you will know that. And if you don't know, try things. Try many things until you find it. Learning new things is very good for our mental wellbeing.

Nature

Twice in my life I've had the privilege to wander in a grove of giant sequoias. Both times were at the same place. Neither time was in the US.

About a hundred years ago someone decided to experiment with planting giant sequoias in Australia. The result of their one-off experiment is a lovely grove of giant sequoias south of Melbourne in Victoria, Australia.

When you step inside the relatively small grove, a stillness settles inside you, mirroring that around you. Everything seems to slow down, sounds are muffled, and time seems to almost stop. It is a similar feeling to the quiet stillness of snowfall in rural places.

I often facilitate groups near the ocean. Several days into a resilience retreat on the beach, and you begin to notice that the group's internal rhythms have shifted. We seem to breathe and move to an internal rhythm that is mirroring that of the ocean waves and tides. At the end of one retreat, a participant said to me, "I've been telling everyone: we go home today. Give whatever you are holding on to, that is holding you back, that is difficult, give it to the ocean before you go. The ocean is big enough to hold it."

Several times in my life I've been privileged enough to watch the sun rise over the Himalaya mountains. It is a breathtaking experience. Viewing the early sunrise over the Annapurnas from the vantage point of the Peace Stupa in Pokhara, Nepal, that same stillness floods both mind and body. I've stood there for long chunks of time, just breathing, my only thought that I simply want to stand there staring at the mountains all day - until I remember the fate of the nice taxi driver waiting for me at the bottom of the mountain.

Forests, snowfall, oceans, mountains, and more. We are part of nature and nature is part of us. Yet we often live our lives thinking we are somehow separate, that nature is to be tamed and controlled and that we can take it or leave it.

For me, nature belongs right in the middle of our conversation about resilience. One of the best things we can do when we're feeling stressed and overwhelmed is to go be in nature. A great way to ground yourself is simply by touching a tree or putting your hands in dirt. Did you know that soil contains natural antidepressant microbes and that working with your hands in soil can help ward off anxiety and depression?

For some of us, like me, this is all logistically harder than for others. When the Covid-19 pandemic began to become serious and limit mobility, I became very jealous of my friends living near natureful places. I began to reflect on how they took that part of their lives for granted while all I wanted to do was to be able to walk outside in nature. Something shifts inside us when we do that, and a deep longing took hold inside of me. I realized that most of my big nature experiences happened when I traveled, which was temporarily no longer an option. So I had to turn even more to bringing nature closer, albeit on a smaller scale.

As you've probably gathered by now, while I live in a concrete jungle metropolis, I'm a born farmer. It's in my blood and was a big part of my growing up. Regardless of where I live, I'll grow something. Urban apartment balconies were meant for plants, and compost, in my humble opinion. There is much to learn from the cycle of growth in nature. There is a different pace and always the promise of beautiful plants from tiny seeds. I want to grow plants that give me joy and also, hopefully, something to add nourishment and flavor to the meals I make for my household. In the end, I just want to grow plants. To get to know them and their peculiarities. To nurture them, learn their cycles, and slow myself down by interacting with their pace of growth.

In many ways, having a garden is all about time and connection. Time to pause and enjoy blooms, to breathe deep and smell herbs, to notice and watch seedlings grow, and to sit with the flow of nature and connect. Connection to nature, to green, to your food source, to growth, to learning the quirks and preferences of each plant and the best way to amend the soil for them, and to other people as you swap plants and knowledge and compost. Connection to yourself - to taking yourself out of yourself, and sitting with your plants and their needs. And connection to creativity - to building beauty and deliciousness with what you have and the satisfaction of growing, harvesting, and enjoying.

As you already know, I've learned a lot from gardening and composting. And you? How do you engage nature in your life? Where do you experience it? How can you bring it closer or be in it more often?

Movement

I grew up in a rural agrarian lifestyle. We were active because there was much to do. When I was younger, we had a large garden in our backyard in which we grew a lot of vegetables for our family consumption. When harvest season came, we canned, froze, and preserved for the winter. There were always chores. Grass needed to be cut, the garden tended, fruits and veggies picked and prepped and stored, dishes washed, the house cleaned, laundry folded, leaves raked, snow shoveled, various things repaired, you name it.

And, of course, we played. Mostly we played outside, making up games and imaginary worlds, riding bikes, sledding, having snowball fights, and tromping through fields or woods around our house.

My paternal grandparents owned a greenhouse. From the time I was old enough and responsible enough, I helped carry plants to customers' cars and held bags while my grandpa shoveled mulch into them for sale from a big mulch pile behind their house, always making sure to secure the twist ties in the precisely correct manner so they would not come undone when the heavy bags were lifted at sale later. When I was old enough, I worked at the greenhouse, which was more or less in operation from March through the first frosts in late fall.

Greenhouse work, if you've never experienced it, includes virtually no sitting down. Seeds need to be planted, seedlings tended and transplanted, hanging baskets and planters

planted, trays and trays and trays of plants moved here and there multiple times as they grow, soil sterilized and mixed properly, flowers deadheaded, and of course endless watering. And then there was the customer service - guiding customers around the greenhouse, answering questions, suggesting plants for their needs, digging pansies out of the beds in which they had wintered over, gathering pots and trays of plants, carrying everything to the front counter for check out, packing it up, and carrying it to customers' cars. On busy days we would grab lunch in small bites as we rushed past the lunch fridge on our way to collect this or that plant or supply being requested by customers. We chewed a slice of apple or a piece of cheese while power walking through the greenhouse carrying many things and dodging many people.

And I loved it.

At school, I was involved with extracurricular activities that mandated movement. I was constantly on the go and moving my body. Rest time, then, was often sedentary time. It may be active, as activities like fishing and creative projects were definitely in the rest category during my childhood, yet it was still more sedentary.

As I became an adult, I began to have a problem. Movement was a way of life. It was something you did for sport or work, not for leisure or fitness. And yet, my life quickly lost the movement-based work and sport as I shifted to desk jobs and no longer had much of an outlet for the sports of my youth.

I needed a mind shift. I still needed to move my body, and eventually I began to understand the seminal significance of movement. Yet my brain kept getting in the way. It was harder to take time and motivate myself to get up and exercise. Work was now sedentary and leisure was movement - a polar shift from my upbringing.

Why is movement important to our resilience?

First, physical health is connected to mental health and both are tied to resilience. One of the best things we can do is take care of our bodies. This includes getting enough sleep, fueling well with nutritious foods, and keeping our bodies fit-ish. Each one of us needs to decide what level of fitness works for us, so I'll leave it at fit-ish.

Second, the stress and trauma we feel is often held in our bodies. We need to shake it out. It is one of the reasons we often feel lighter after doing some exercise during particularly stressful or difficult times in our lives and why we feel grumpy and short tempered if we haven't moved in too long. If you want to learn more about how our bodies hold trauma and stress, check out the many resources on somatic approaches to therapy.

Third, movement creates movement and energy. Movement is one clear way to stoke the spark and flame inside of us. The more we do it, the more energy we have to do it more, and the more energy we have for other things as well. In many ways, movement can be an active power plant to help us recharge our batteries.

Of course, none of this means we need to all become pro athletes in order to have good resilience practice. Movement can be small, low impact, and shorter than we think. Sometimes we get stuck on the idea that it always has to be big, that it always has to be long and super hard. As with most things in resilience practice, it is more about the consistency than the intensity.

Perhaps unsurprisingly, different kinds of movement work for different people. Some of us absolutely love running. That's not me. I do it sometimes because it's supposed to be good for me - and I usually feel good after. But I don't enjoy the process and my body wasn't built to run. Some of us like solo movement while others of us like to move with other people. Some of us prefer something more artistic, like dancing, while others of us prefer to chase a ball or play a team sport. It doesn't matter what it is, as long as we are moving.

So what does consistency instead of intensity in movement really look like? During the pandemic, almost all of my facilitation work shifted to be online. As part of different sessions, I facilitated short dance parties for many different groups. After the initial embarrassment and laughing and terror, the end result was always the same. Even one song was enough to help groups feel lighter, more energized, and more connected to each other. The effect was amplified if we managed more than one song.

At the end, I always asked how the group was feeling. And then we'd talk about why we don't do this more often. What stops us from taking five minutes in the middle of our day, turning on our favorite song, and dancing like no one is watching? Especially if we're working from home?

At this point I'd like to give a shout out and kudos to all the people on all the calls who found themselves in public spaces, like their offices, and still chose to dance anyway. You're all champs.

I facilitated a resilience session recently where one participant set a goal of finding joy in movement. She said that she had previously set a goal around exercise and was now exercising every day as a habit. While she was happy with how that was going, she wasn't finding any joy in it. She was working out because she knew it was good for her. Now she wanted to find joy in movement as well.

Sometimes taking care of ourselves means doing things we don't really want to do and don't really enjoy. It means exercising even though we'd rather not. It means going to bed early instead of staying up to watch the next episode of a show we are into. And it can also mean finding joy in these things as well. After all, there's nothing quite like snuggling into a freshly made bed with crisp, clean sheets. Or prolonging the enjoyment of the experience of a TV show by extending our viewing over the course of days or weeks rather than simply binge watching to get it done. Somehow it comes back around to intention and mindfulness in what we focus on.

How do you like to move? How can you make sure you do it regularly?

Connection

When the Covid-19 pandemic started getting serious, a friend of mine who is well trained in somatic approaches started a virtual dance party group. Five times a day anyone could log in for 20 minutes of dancing. No talking. Just dancing freestyle. When it was time to start, the DJ for the session would say welcome and would start the music. Everyone muted their Zoom and left their cameras on. And we danced. Good, bad, ugly, it didn't matter. As long as you were dancing. Each session ended with the same song about resilience. Only then did we unmute and quickly introduce ourselves and where we were dancing. That was it.

My friend knew the importance of movement during stressful times. She also knew the importance of connection and community. As the group got going, something happened in perhaps an unexpected way. Those of us who became regulars suddenly felt closer to each other than we thought possible. Many of us had never met and didn't know each other before we started dancing together virtually. Yet the connection was real and tangible.

Most of the interactions we have in life are transactional in nature and it can lead to an ignoring or forgetting of the importance of real connection.

Think about it. You grab your morning coffee from your usual place on the way to work. You may not even look the seller in the eye as you try to manage too many things in your hands at once while attempting to keep everything moving quickly. Many of our conversations at home are about transactional things: what's for dinner, who is going to stop and pick up that needed item tomorrow, have you changed the dead lightbulb yet. Even with our friends, often our conversations are more transactional.

And in our world of chat, it's even worse. Have you ever had a friend chat you on some platform or other and start sharing about a crisis in their life? They are pouring their heart out to you via chat while you respond nicely with the appropriate crying, heart, hug, etc. emojis and short, predictable phrases, all while you are simultaneously doing something else entirely. Is it connection? I'm not so sure.

When was the last time you actually connected deeply with someone? When you had a conversation the primary goal of which was for each of you to be seen and heard and understood by the other, and for no one to try to solve any problems or fix anything. When you walked away feeling deep inside that these goals had been realized - that you had deeply seen, heard, and understood each other. Perhaps, later, the conversation had wandered into problem solving or brainstorming. But it started with complete and deep understanding.

When I think about this, I always think about my friend I mentioned in the section on intention. She is excellent at this. Regardless of how many other things she is juggling, she has the ability to focus on each conversation, making you feel like you are the only thing going on for her right now. It is intention and it is connection. For that conversation, she is solely focused on the here and now and seeing, hearing, and understanding what you are saying. And it is beautiful and life giving.

I'm not saying that every interaction we have each day must include some deep connection. Yet if we are not intentional about it, we can all too easily lose those moments of real connection in our lives almost entirely. How can we be intentional about ensuring we actually connect to someone or someones regularly in our lives? What does it take to have this sort of connecting conversation?

First, unsurprisingly, it takes intention. It takes intention to focus on the other person and not to be distracted, to be mindful and present. Then, it takes deep listening. The kind of listening that is to understand rather than to respond or fix or judge. And it takes this from all parties to the conversation.

This sort of interaction takes practice.

Often in sessions I facilitate, we talk about the difference between debate, discussion, and dialogue. The goal of debate is to win. I'm right, you're wrong. And there are places and spaces where we need this skill and this kind of interaction.

Mostly in our lives we find ourselves in discussion. The word discussion comes from a Latin root word that means "to break apart". This is exactly what a discussion is and does. We break apart a topic into different components, perspectives, and ideas. Then we seek to form some of those parts into a decision or way forward or some sort of agreement. This is probably the most used of the three in our workplaces, and perhaps also in the rest of our lives as well.

Dialogue, on the other hand, in its purest form has one, deceptively simple, goal: to understand. While dialogue is often used as a tool in a larger process seeking some result, at its core is just this simple purpose. Real dialogue means I'm here to understand you fully and for you to understand me. There's no judgment. I don't have to agree with you. At the end, we don't have to agree on a way forward or a common understanding of an issue. I simply need to understand your perspectives deeply - what you think, how you got to that understanding, and why you hold that perspective. And you simply need to do the same for me.

This is easy with easy things. The more sensitive or hot the topic, the harder this is to do. Our human nature of trying to convince the other person that we are right and get them to agree can be hard to overcome. Also, our judgment voice disagreeing with the opinions of the other person can be equally hard to sideline. Yet in dialogue we must temporarily suspend moral judgment and focus solely on understanding.

A dialogue-type conversation, then, can set us up well for deep connection. We don't interrupt. We don't counter each other.

We don't jump in with our own related story. We ask open questions from a place of curiosity, prompting the other person to tell us more and deepen our understanding. We phrase our questions well, so that instead of "How could you possibly think that?" we ask, "What in your experience has led you to that opinion?" Instead of "But don't you think..." or "Wouldn't you agree..." we ask, "What do you think of this other perspective?"

This sort of conversation takes practice. And it seems we as a global society are increasingly losing the ability to communicate in this way around flashpoint issues. To me, that means we need to practice it all the more. We can start on topics that are less volatile to hone our skills, and then slowly move to other topics we care more about or are more passionate about.

The point in all of this, of course, is connection. Even if we disagree fundamentally about something, we can still be friends, family, and colleagues and this becomes easier if we have connected, if we understand each other on a deeper level. We can disagree and still respect each other and continue a relationship.

And even if we do agree, we still need to be seen and heard and understood by others. And we need to see, hear, and understand them too. Some conversations need to be about connection beyond the transactional.

Community

Years ago when I lived in Chicago, I found myself at an international folk dancing group. How did I get there? The usual way, I guess. A friend of mine was soon to move to work with Roma people in the Czech Republic and wanted to learn some things about Roma culture. A friend of hers invited her to the international folk dancing group, as some of the dances in the regular lineup were Roma. My friend didn't want to go alone and asked me to go with her. Isn't that the random way so many of our stories start?

Thus we found ourselves walking into the room one Monday night to be immediately greeted with enthusiasm and warmth. The group dances for several hours every Monday night, and my friend never went again. I, on the other hand, joined the group. Go figure.

I learned about international folk dancing and that there are groups around the world who gather to dance regularly. Dances mostly hail from places like Romania, Greece, Israel, the Roma culture, Serbia, Albania, Turkey, Macedonia, Hungary, Bulgaria, the Kurdish culture, France, Croatia, and more. They are pieces of culture that have been passed down through generations and carried along as people moved around the world. Many dances are done in a circle or a line with the dancers all holding hands or shoulders, or linking arms or hanging on to their neighbors' belt. Yes, some people intentionally bring belts just for this purpose.

The group I joined is probably typical - a hodgepodge of people with different backgrounds who somehow found their way to this pastime, be it through birth or curiosity. Some had been dancing all their lives, which is considerable given that most were in their 50s, 60s, 70s, and 80s.

What I found was both connection and community. Some people were skilled dancers, others not so much. And no one cared. Those hanging around the edges of the dancing circle were always pulled in to join the group. If the dance was more difficult and they were learning, someone would join them behind the main line to help them get the steps before pulling them in to join the rest of the group. Some people, even after years of regular attendance, couldn't ever quite get the steps right to just about everything. But no one really cared. As we all got older, some people's previously clean stepping became more shuffled and less bouncy.

Again, it didn't matter. We held hands as we danced. If you lost your balance, your neighbors would help hold you up. If you lost the rhythm, your neighbors were there for that too. If you wanted to dance in a faster or slower line, no worries, someone would join you.

What mattered was being there, joining the line, and moving along to music that resonated somewhere deep inside and practically told your feet what to do next. And then the Covid-19 pandemic came.

Obviously regular folk dancing together in a group of older people inside and holding hands was quickly canceled as the pandemic came into full swing. I started to wonder how they were all doing - I'd long since moved to Bangkok and missed dancing with the group. Then I got a message through the group's email list. They were going to dance virtually. Same time as usual, but now on Zoom.

It was exciting for me as it meant I could dance with them again, so I joined as much as I was able. People joined from all over the world and they actually expanded their reach far and wide. They would play the songs and we would all dance, cameras on, in our homes. They would teach new dances, review old ones, celebrate birthdays, and have certain times for chit chat - just like if you were there together in the room.

A couple months into the pandemic, I asked some of the group how they were doing. The answer? They were thriving. They were now dancing every day as other groups also went virtual. They danced with people all over the world at different times seven days a week. And they were loving it.

I also observed some other things. There was always some catching up and conversation among those there early. During the pandemic, this conversation included checking on each other, especially those with less mobility or less support nearby. "Do you have what you need? No? Ok, no problem. We'll drop off a grocery delivery with the supplies you need to you tomorrow. We'll put it on your porch and ring your doorbell and walk away." The community came together to help each other through.

As the pandemic eased, the group began to dance again in person. And they also kept their virtual presence. Dancing became a hybrid event. I can still join, and now I get to dance with all the others who are either at home or in the room together. It's rather like dancing behind the line again.

Community. We all need it. No one gets to where they are by themselves. We've all had others helping us, pushing us, supporting us, and opening doors.

How aware are we of our community? How much do we know and recognize who they are? You can start by answering this question: who do you support and who supports you?

For some of us, life is a bit more lonely or disconnected. Perhaps we live outside of our original community. Perhaps we are in professional roles that are more individual, like CEOs or entrepreneurs who don't exactly have peers in their organizations. For us, we have to create our community. We have to be more intentional about surrounding ourselves with folks who we support and who support us. And then we have to be intentional about engaging with them, checking in on each other, offering help, and also asking for it.

Who is your community? Who do you support and who supports you? How can you be intentional about cultivating the community you need?

Chapter 7
Stir Periodically & Monitor Dampness

*"You can't go back and change the beginning,
but you can start where you are and change the ending."*
- C.S. Lewis

As you nurture your compost system, you'll have to stir it periodically. If you have a tumbler, that means having some fun by spinning the tumbler like a game show contestant. I

must admit that when I did have a tumbler, this part of things often had me giggling with glee. It's just fun.

You'll also have to monitor the amount of moisture in the mix. If it's too dry, it will stagnate and you won't get the necessary decomposition. If it's too wet, it will just be a muddy, glumpy mess that also won't digest properly.

The good news is that this balance is more or less easily maintained. If you stir your compost and find that it is too dry, add some more green matter or plain water. If it's too wet, add some more brown material.

Every composting system balances a bit differently. When I first started with the buckets, the ideal ratio was about one part green to two parts brown material. Later, I had a tumbler for a while that seemed to run on the wet side so I needed a lot more brown material to keep it in balance. Now, my stacked ceramic tier runs much more on the dry side depending on how much sun and rain it comes in contact with. I find it easier to balance than the tumbler as I tend to have more green (wet) than brown (dry) compostable material and it's easy to just add a splash of water if it needs it.

Like our compost, our resilience practice also needs some monitoring and balancing. Elements in our lives fluctuate regularly. In the same way I need to monitor my compost and consider the impact of sun and rain on my ceramic tier system as I keep the mix in balance, I also need to monitor my resilience muscle, resilience practice, and life balance amidst fluctuating life circumstances.

The Only Constant is Change

If you delve into the cupboards of my kitchen, you'll find a plethora of plastic and glass storage containers, leftovers bowls, and jars - many with nicely locking lids. You also might notice that some have writing on them that does not in any way reflect anything about their contents. There's one that says "salt", for instance, that never holds anything remotely like salt. Then there's one that says Starbucks, and while sometimes it does hold coffee grounds, it's not Starbucks.

Of course what's happened is that we decided to store something in a particular container, like the salt, and so someone in my household decided to label it - a very helpful notion. Writing SALT in large letters with a nice, permanent Sharpie pen directly onto the container lid is indeed rather satisfying.

The problem is that some time later something changed and we moved the storage of the salt to a different sort of container. Now we've got a container labeled salt and actual salt in a different container. Come to think of it, the current salt container has no label at all.

As our labeled and mis-labeled containers began to become a bit confusing, I realized it was only going to get worse as the cycle of organizing and reorganizing our storage of kitchen and food items continued.

As a facilitator, one of the main supplies I use constantly, aside from good markers, is masking tape. Masking tape comes in many widths, holds just fine for my purposes, and generally does not strip paint off walls when removed at the end of a workshop. Various rolls of masking tape of different widths can always be found in my office, my house, and my bags.

Thus, when next it came time to label another storage container, I grabbed a roll of masking tape along with that satisfying Sharpie marker. Now in my kitchen you'll mostly find our containers with labels written on masking tape. They stay long term, are clear and easy to read, and so work in all ways possible. And, when the inevitable change comes, they are easy to remove and adjust as needed. If the only constant in life and storage containers is change, then we are prepared to adjust with it.

If you are one of those people who has a solid and stalwart morning routine that you almost never have to compromise, I salute you and I'm a bit jealous. Whether we admit it or not, in life, the only constant is, indeed, change. We sometimes succeed in fooling ourselves that things are just the same as they always have been, and it's never actually true.

In resilience practice, this can have far reaching impacts. Imagine that you have found the practices that work for you. You have put in place a routine that works well and you are feeling great. Then something changes. Maybe you get a new job that requires you to leave for work earlier, throwing off your morning routine. Maybe you get injured or sick and can't pursue that physical activity you have been leaning on. Maybe you've been building your resilience practice well for years and suddenly things start to feel stale. Life changes in so many big and small ways, and we also change along with it. What happens to your resilience practice when things change?

In my case, the nature of change in my life is daily, making this problem even more acute. When I started to work on my resilience practice, I had a more or less predictable job in many ways. Barring emergencies, which happened a couple times per year, I went to the office at regular times, five days a week. Later, I left that job and started my own social enterprise doing facilitation, resilience, peacebuilding, leadership development, and accompaniment. Suddenly my days were unpredictable.

There is no regular day in my work schedule and no two days are the same. This became even more pronounced as everything went online in response to the pandemic. I've facilitated online at four in the morning or until after midnight. Some days I can control, more or less, when meetings are scheduled. Other days find me facilitating all day or multi-day events off site. I often facilitate around the country, region, and worldwide. All attempts at a regular morning routine are always disrupted by my unpredictable schedule.

To start working on this dilemma, I hold on to this quote: "Be stubborn about your goals and flexible about your methods."

Seeking some way to tame this constant shifting, I read about people who plan their week in advance. It sounded cool, so I tried it. It didn't work. A day into the week and things had already shifted, throwing my plans out of whack again. I think my record for the shortest time my week plan lasted was a couple hours, the longest was a bit over a day. And then I had to replan everything, probably not for the last time. So I went even smaller, I planned each day the night before. Now this is part of my practice.

First I needed to get my head straight about priorities. I'm a morning person, so I always thought I should work most in the morning when I'm at my best. That meant pushing my exercise or movement for the day to later, when it would be easier to make excuses and skip it. While I love to be active, exercising is one of the first things I skip when I get busy or don't feel like it. I'm still reprogramming my brain, which may well be a lifelong endeavor. This pattern of easy excuses for not exercising reared its ugly head strongly and I fought it and myself for a while.

Then I tried something different. I put my daily movement earlier in my schedule plan. I put it for when I'm at my best. Grounded in the truth that taking care of myself well is the best thing I can do for my work, I finally put myself first in my schedule. I realized I'd been saying this all along while still missing the mark for myself.

It was a game changer. Initially I was worried that it would mean doing most of my work in times when I'm not at my peak, but that didn't happen. Instead, the positive benefits of movement and exercise made it so that the hours immediately after that I had designated as working time were more productive and efficient.

Every evening I plan my next day. I have puzzle pieces I fit together of how I want to design that day. When will I work, when do I have meetings, when will I sleep, what chores will I do around the house, when will I move, when will I cook and eat, and when will I do what resilience practice activity or activities?

I've tried many tools to help me do this, mostly digital tools. At the moment, I'm using Owaves, a visually appealing app that allows you to drop in different pieces of life for each day. When I found it, it was exactly what I needed. There are many customizable options in the app, and when I began using it they were only available on the phone version of the app. Unaware of this, I downloaded the tablet version, enjoying the larger display of the attractive interface. Unknowingly stuck with limited options, I assumed that was how the app was designed and found the best way to make it work for me. Now I'm rather attached to the stripped down version. It's just enough structure in my day to keep me on track, but not too much so that I feel restricted. It helps me keep on the flow that I want for each day.

Owaves is a big reason that this book even got written at all. It had been in progress at some stage or other for a long time and I struggled, like many, to make real, tangible strides. I recommitted to writing daily, even just for a short time. And what kept me going with this commitment was planning my day in a way that worked for me and then actively using that plan to help me do what I needed to do, especially when it came to resilience practice and those other things that are important that generally are forced to take a back seat to things that present themselves as urgent. In the struggle between the urgent and the important, getting my head straight about priorities and planning my days using a tool that worked for me changed everything.

None of this is to say that this is the only way. As always, we all must find the methods and tools that work for us. So go looking for them and try things out. Someone else somewhere out there has had the same struggle you are having, and hopefully has created a tool or app or approach to help. All you have to do is find it.

Of course not all of us have high levels of freedom in planning the bulk of our days. I work for myself, which gives me a lot of that freedom. I used to work in many jobs that did not have any of this sort of flexibility at all and in which I felt nervous and afraid if the line at the coffee place was too long, meaning I might be gone from my desk a minute or two over the allowed break time.

To be honest, while I didn't know it at the time, I started to think about my approach to resilience practice while in one of those jobs. If you had asked me then, I wouldn't have known or had the language to properly explain it, but I was already seeking better balance and mental health. If that is you, it's ok. How can you plan the parts of your day that you do control? How can you better approach the parts in which you have less control? A big piece of all of this is what you do, and perhaps an even bigger piece is the mindset and perspective you hold.

The other part of maintaining resilience practice when the only constant in life is change, is to know that you may need to update it from time to time. We change, life changes, and what has been working for you before may no longer work for you at some point in the future. Exploring and trying new things is excellent for our mental health and something that we all need to do from time to time in terms of our resilience practice. Think about it as an adventure instead of approaching potential change with dismay. Experiment to find what works for you.

Grounding

If change is the norm, how can we stay grounded even in the midst of upheaval? We can start with figuring out what grounds us to begin with.

In psychological first aid, grounding is a technique to help us calm down when we are in an acute state of stress. It might include things like touching a wall or a tree, taking a drink of water, tuning in to our senses, or planting our feet firmly on the floor or directly on the ground. Grounding settles us through reconnecting us to the tangible.

Staying grounded, then, reconnects us to our roots - to who we are and our purpose, or what Simon Sinek calls our Why. So what grounds you? What reconnects you to who you are and why you are here on this earth? Those things that keep us grounded might include people, convictions, memories, items, or activities.

Like many aspects of resilience, we read these questions and assume we know the answers. Yet often when we need to draw on them the most, they elude us. We need to do some self learning, identify what grounds us, and bring that knowledge from our subconscious into our conscious minds. Then, when we need it most, we know exactly where to turn and what to do.

The other thing I find useful is to intentionally take moments to reconnect with my roots - my identities and my why. We needn't wait for crises to reconnect. We should regularly maintain those connections, keeping them as robust as possible and strengthening our tether to what matters to us. Not only does this reinforce the courage of our convictions, it also lessens the ease and frequency at which we may find ourselves floating and lost.

In the midst of the constant change that is life, we must remain rooted in who we are and why we are here, giving space for our many facets and needs. We have purpose and we need to also take care of ourselves. How do we choose and balance between hustling for why we are here, living lives of meaning, and resilience practice? What does it even mean to live a life of meaning and purpose?

> The Summer Day by Mary Oliver
>
> Who made the world?
> Who made the swan, and the black bear?
> Who made the grasshopper?
> This grasshopper, I mean—
> the one who has flung herself out of the grass, the one who is eating sugar out of my hand, who is moving her jaws back and forth instead of up and down—
> who is gazing around with her enormous and complicated eyes.

> Now she lifts her pale forearms and thoroughly
> washes her face.
> Now she snaps her wings open, and floats away.
> I don't know exactly what a prayer is.
> I do know how to pay attention, how to fall down
> into the grass, how to kneel down in the grass, how
> to be idle and blessed, how to stroll through the
> fields, which is what I have been doing all day.
> Tell me, what else should I have done?
> Doesn't everything die at last, and too soon?
> Tell me, what is it you plan to do
> with your one wild and precious life?

There's the oft quoted line: "What is it you plan to do with your one wild and precious life?" At first glance, it could be seen as pointing to a life of hustling to do something somehow deemed as worthy. But it's not.

Mary Oliver's own answer to this question was to wander in nature and notice things. If life's meaning is in the living, where would you like to find it? How can you ground yourself in the qualities of the living itself rather than pinning your worth to accomplishments? If wandering in nature and noticing is a worthwhile life pursuit, what does that mean for your own life?

Limit Yourself

Yes, you read that right. One of the books that has shifted my thinking in essential and fundamental ways is *Four Thousand*

Weeks: Time Management for Mortals by Oliver Burkeman. Of the many existential nuggets in his book, I'd like to highlight this one here: limit yourself.

In his book, Burkeman talks about limiting the time we take for certain tasks.

As I said, I started writing this book a long time ago. I'd work on it sporadically, always waiting for the right moment, whatever that undefined utopian imaginary state meant, and never really making much progress. I'd plan chunks of time here and there to work on it, and then find myself sitting staring at the blank page on the screen trying to gather my thoughts. Needless to say, and perhaps predictably, it wasn't really working.

Then I changed my approach. Most writers will tell you that consistency is the key. Whether you write for 10 minutes or 10 hours at a time, the important thing is to do it consistently. Burkeman adds to that thought with his principle of radical incrementalism. If you set out to do something, in this case write, for 30 minutes a day, let's say, then stop when your30 minutes are up. Don't give in to the temptation to keep going because you are on a roll or things are flowing well as it will turn into sabotage later. He writes:

> The psychology professor Robert Boice spent his career studying the writing habits of his fellow academics, reaching the conclusion that the most productive and successful among them generally made writing a smaller part of their daily routine than the others,

so that it was much more feasible to keep going with it day after day. They cultivated the patience to tolerate the fact that they probably wouldn't be producing very much on any individual day, with the result that they produced much more over the long term. They wrote in brief daily sessions — sometimes as short as ten minutes, and never longer than four hours — and they religiously took weekends off. The panicked PhD students in whom Boice tried to inculcate this regimen rarely had the forbearance to hear it. They had looming deadlines, they protested, and couldn't afford such self-indulgent work habits. They needed their dissertations finished, and fast! But for Boice, that reaction just proved his point. It was precisely the students' impatient desire to hasten their work beyond its appropriate pace, to race on to the point of completion, that was impeding their progress. They couldn't stand the discomfort that arose from being forced to acknowledge their limited control over the speed of the creative process — and so they sought to escape it, either by not getting down to work at all, or by rushing headlong into stressful all-day writing binges, which led to procrastination later on, because it made them learn to hate the whole endeavor.

One critical aspect of the radical incrementalist approach, which runs counter to much mainstream advice on productivity, is thus to be willing to stop when your daily time is up, even when you're bursting with energy and feel as though you could get much more done. If you've decided to work on a given project for fifty minutes, then once fifty minutes have elapsed, get up and walk away from it. Why? Because as Boice explained, the urge to push onward beyond that point "includes a big component of impatience about not being finished, about not being productive enough, about never again finding such an ideal time" for work. Stopping helps strengthen the muscle of patience that will permit you to return to the project again and again, and thus to sustain your productivity over an entire career."

I can corroborate Burkeman's point. This approach is how this book got written. I'm convinced that it is the only way that could have happened as all my previous attempts had failed. It was a game changer for me.

In the past, I would organize my efforts for everything and anything, not just writing this book, by simply doing something until either it was finished or other commitments forced me to stop for the moment or day. As I reflect back, I realize that approach only served to tire me out and make me less excited about continuing the work again the next day. As I used the radical incrementalism approach in the writing of this book, I found myself excited to write each day, words spilling out onto the page.

As I got deeper into this book, it started to occupy ever increasing amounts of my thoughts. I was sorely tempted over and over again to increase my daily writing time or return to working on this book again later in the day. It took some discipline to resist these urges, but I stuck to the principle of radical incrementalism and both the book and I are better for it.

If you've made it this far and you haven't yet picked up a copy of *Four Thousand Weeks*, do it now, right now, and enjoy the read.

What does all of this mean for resilience? I argue that the principle of radical incrementalism is as applicable to resilience as it is to writing and anything else important. Put limits on your resilience practice. Do things for a predetermined amount of time and then stop and do something else in your day. This process can help us bring intention and focus. It can help us make that limited time all the more meaningful and effective.

Now that this book is written, I'll be exploring more courageously how the principle of radical incrementalism can impact other areas of my life.

Build Your Path Well

Since I came out of burnout those years ago, I've found myself at times slipping back down into it. Just because you are actively pursuing resilience doesn't mean things will always be moving in a positive direction. We are still susceptible to backsliding, lapses, falling out of balance without realizing it, and shock events in our lives.

These days, I'm more attuned to it and pay better attention

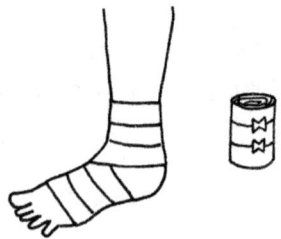

to the warning signs that I'm out of balance or losing my footing. When I realize I'm slipping, I'm now more able to reach out and grab on to the supports I've put in place along the path I'm building towards resilience. I can more easily find grounding and footing and continue the baby steps that will lead me in a positive direction.

Every time I slip, it reinforces to me the necessity of strengthening my resilience muscles and building my path well. It seems that life is a never ending series of ups and downs, and at any given moment I can find myself at any point from the top of a mountain to the bottom of a hole or somewhere in between. This is why resilience is a life-long practice. We will always need it. And it helps us stay out of many of the deep holes we might otherwise have fallen into. It is the consistent, daily baby steps that keep us going as inspired and creative people.

Beginning Again ... And Again

I have weak ankles. It's just in my genes. One of the regular patterns in my life is that just about the time when I'm feeling good and strong and fit with whatever I'm doing for exercise, I'll twist or turn or sprain an ankle badly. Of course. And then I'll have to rest it a bit while it heals, watching my habits and fitness level fall away.

Once my ankle heals, it's time to start again. While my performance level will invariably be less than when I sustained the injury, I'm not starting from nothing. I'm starting from experience and muscle memory. And so I begin again. Resilience is the same.

Since we can expect to find ourselves on a constant journey up and down between the high and low moments of our lives with disruptions to our preferred routines a regular occurrence, it means that along the way we'll need to start over again and again.

Referring to the process of writing, Kevin Ashton said, "Nothing begins good, but everything good begins. Everything can be revised, erased, or rearranged later. The courage of creation is making bad beginnings." I think this applies to resilience too. We can feel intimidated and anxious about getting started, wondering if we'll put a foot wrong or if what we are planning will have any impact at all. The point is to begin, and to keep beginning again as you need to. Every time you begin again, you don't start from zero, you start from experience.

I've begun and begun again in my resilience practice many times. My paths up and down between the highs and lows of life are well hewn and trod. And even still, sometimes I need to take time to wipe my eyes of dust and clear my head of cobwebs to realize I've slid back a bit and am out of balance. Sometimes I need to pay closer attention to my compost, stirring it more, being more intentional about what I put into it, tracking the moisture levels more closely, and more actively adjusting to bring it back in balance.

Maintaining your resilience is rather like gardening. You can plant the perfect garden, but it won't remain that way without the attention of weeding, watering, and generally tending it. Sometimes I find I've neglected my resilience muscles, and then I recommit and begin again, making those small daily choices that will build my life toward resilience.

Chapter 8
Curing: Fermentation Takes Time & Space

"...it's virtually guaranteed that truly stopping to rest - as opposed to training for a 10K, or heading off on a meditation retreat with the goal of attaining spiritual enlightenment - is initially going to provoke serious feelings of discomfort, rather than of delight.
That discomfort isn't a sign that you shouldn't be doing it, though. It's a sign that you definitely should."
- Oliver Burkeman, Four Thousand Weeks:
Time Management for Mortals

Baby Steps

Angela Duckworth has said, "Life is more about consistency than about intensity. Intensity steals the limelight." In other words, baby steps every day. I've used the phrase baby steps throughout this book, and this is why.

When you're deep into burnout, or other significant life disruptions for that matter, finding your way out all but seems impossible and any progress you make seems insignificant. Like all big things, it is difficult to do, so we must keep a longer term perspective. We must hold on to the absolute belief that each little choice we make, each baby step, every day, will lead us where we want to go. That after some time passes, we will turn around, look back, and see that our path has been paved by all those small moments.

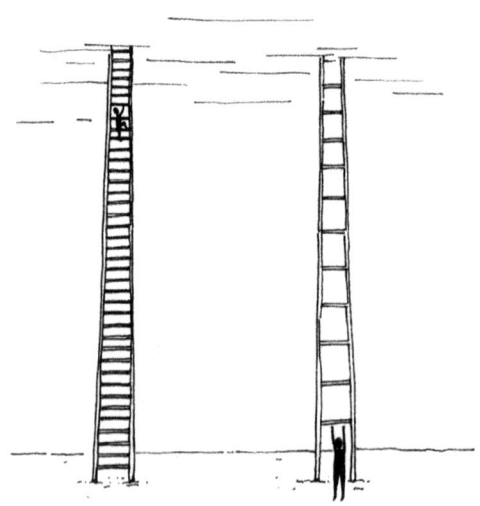

It isn't about big and fast. In fact, there's nothing fast about this. And yes, I definitely feel the frustration around that. If I know what I need to do to help heal myself, my immediate mindset will always be: ok, let's do it! Heal. Now! But it doesn't work that way.

The only way anything great and wonderful has ever happened has been through a long road of baby steps. Often we are witness to merely the final one or two steps of the shuffling journey someone has walked. And we then have the impression that this wonderful thing happened quickly and easily for that person. Of course we're wrong. We're witnessing the culmination of hours and days and weeks and years of small choices every day.

In my own journey, many times I look at where I am, I know what I need to do, and I'm discouraged at the seemingly monumental task ahead of me in all its creeping slowness and the seeming insignificance of the simple choice in front of me at that moment. It helps if I shift my mindset.

Instead of endlessly staring at the long way I have to go to get to where I think I want to be in life, focusing on the limited size of my possible daily steps, I try to shift my perspective to focus on the choices I make each day. Once I make the choice that will take me in the direction I'm currently seeking, I take a moment to reflect on it, feel good about it, and mentally tick off another step.

It sounds nice to write that, and some days I'm more successful at it than others. I think somewhere inside we humans all just want the shortcut. Why can't I go from zero to hero in a day? I mean, training montages in movies only last a couple of minutes. It's hard to celebrate those super small baby steps.

Perhaps a big part of the non-glitzy nature of my own resilience journey has been to grapple with the finite limitations of being human and to make peace with the slow but steady pace that really holds life together. I find this can be especially hard when living in the midst of a hustle culture and a society that prioritizes all things fast and instant gratification.

Frustratingly, the baby step journey is never linear. It will never lay out the smoothest and most direct path. Yes, you will make detours. You will take a few steps back sometimes. And each choice is an opportunity to take another step forward. Yet, as this poem from Ruth Feldman helps me remember, sometimes detours were the way I was supposed to go all along.

>Detour, by Ruth Feldman
>
>I took a long time getting here,
>Much of it wasted on wrong turns,
>Back roads riddled by ruts.
>I had adventures
>I never would have known
>If I proceeded as the crow flies.
>Super highways are so sure
>Of where they are going:
>They arrive too soon.

A straight line isn't always
The shortest distance
Between two people.
Sometimes I act as though
I'm heading somewhere else
While, imperceptibly,
I narrow the gap between you and me.
I'm not sure I'll ever
Know the right way, but I don't mind
Getting lost now and then.
Maps don't know everything.

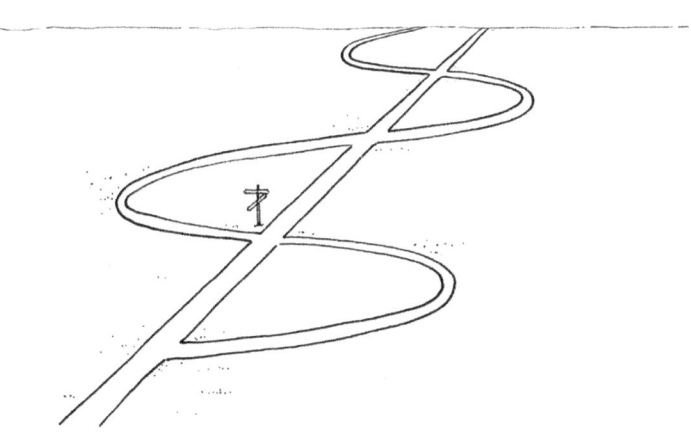

Rest & Wasting Time

"Rest is not idleness, and to lie sometimes on the grass on a summer day listening to the murmur of water, or watching the clouds float across the sky, is hardly a waste of time."
- John Lubbock

Let's take a pause. As we walk through all these topics and approaches, it may seem to sound like a lot of doing. Just another form of hustle.

And that's not what it is.

Rest is essential. Slowing down is essential. Taking moments to breathe, to live for the now without the many distractions that constantly congest our headspace, is essential. To sleep well and enough daily and not just on weekends is essential. To not engage in resilience practices because we think we should or need to or to check it off our to-do list, but rather because we want to, and we've decided to use that time in this way is the point.

Remember aimless time? For me, aimless time is also related to wasting time. When I work with groups, I'll often try to include some element of wasting time together, even if it is in short moments. In the preparatory meeting for our upcoming work session, it is usually not the first thing I tell people we're going to do. You can imagine the reactions if it was. See, I've learned something they may not know yet. I've learned that wasting time together is never time wasted. It is always valuable. The output isn't something you can hold in your hand. It is something you hold in your being and in your relationships. Like the song says, "The greatest things you'll ever know are invisible." That's the space in which I work. And that's where you find resilience work and the beauties of wasting time together.

Personally, I think wasting time individually is generally not wasted either. Like with aimless time, often I find my brain, perhaps my subconscious, processing or working through something while I'm wasting time. I don't always know what it is, but I can feel it happening. I'm composting.

And of course there's a link between rest and wasting time, as rest is also never time wasted. We need to think again about how we conceptualize productivity and meaning. Alan Watts said, "Stop measuring days by degrees of productivity and start experiencing them by degrees of presence."

We tend to measure our days by how productive we have been - how many worthwhile things we've accomplished each day. Time, after all, is money, and the point is to always get more of it. But is it? Is time really money always, or even at all? Is the true measure of a day a list of outputs? Personally, I don't think so.

Some years ago, John Paul Lederach challenged himself to include more mindfulness and reflection into his days. He wanted to take note of those beautiful and special moments each day that make you catch your breath in wonder and awe. Maybe it is something beautiful you see, something yummy you taste, something enticing you smell, or something kind you observe someone doing for someone else. John Paul was already an avid haikuist. So his challenge to himself was to notice life more intentionally and write one haiku a day for a year capturing those special, noticed moments.

Why haiku? As John Paul said at an On Being Gathering in 2018:

> Near the end of his life, Bashō said, "Across all these years, I have only written but four or five haikus." What an extraordinary thing to say, for a man who probably could write 15 or 20 in a single morning, who practiced it for decades. I've often wondered what he might have meant. Perhaps it's this — that he understood haiku as a practice, that was to notice the ways that you might capture the wonder of the human experience in the simplest of terms. It combines the beginner's mind — what we might call joy, with ancient wisdom — what we might call patience. How do you hold joy and patience, particularly when things fall apart and harm burrows in?
>
> At a certain time in my peacebuilding journey, sitting close to and with human suffering, little by little I was experiencing a deadening of my soul. Sometimes we call this "burnout." The ancestor presence of Bashō arrived unexpectedly. It's amazing how something you learn in the second grade could become the light that enlivens the spirit. As an adult second-grader, my rediscovery was in understanding haiku as a contemplative practice, the seeking of the haiku attitude;

that is, to prepare yourself to be touched by beauty, the noticing of the haiku moment that is the aha when the world is revealed for what it is — and that simple form, that five-seven-five that was landed on and experienced because it could be said in a single breath. So I started writing haiku, and I never stopped — finger-tapping choreography of life. If you ever see me walking, and you see me tapping, it's because there are haikus all around you.

Over time, I found that haiku was a traveling compass that holds a very strange needle. It's not interested in north. It spins wildly, as long as you busy your way through life, and it only slows and points when you slow enough to notice. I'm learning
to listen in haiku.

John Paul was the one who introduced, or I should say re-introduced, me to haiku. He started it all. Hearing John Paul talk about his year-long haiku challenge resonated with me and came back to my mind some years after. I was thinking about how to add more reflection and mindfulness into my life while also noticing more and paying attention to those moments - those haiku moments. So I decided to take on the challenge myself: one haiku a day for a year. As I'm writing this, that was five years ago. Needless to say, I not only successfully completed my year, but I'm still going. I just can't stop.

I try to listen to the haiku moments in each day. Sometimes when I get to the end of the day without one in mind, I sit and reflect on the day itself. What was the point? What was important? And that nugget becomes my haiku for that day.

Thousands of days and haiku later, the same lesson John Paul talks about emerged for me from an observation. The days with long productivity lists and lots of hustle where I've busied my way through life, to borrow John Paul's phrase, don't usually bring good haiku reflections. When I sit and reflect on the day, I see a list in my mind. Sometimes it is hard to find the haiku moment there. It seems on those days that I didn't slow enough to notice, so my haiku compass struggled to point to anything.

On the other hand, days with rest or wasting time or resilience practice or slowing down somewhere in them bring the most insightful haiku - the days when I've slowed enough to notice.

It doesn't have to be this or that, all or nothing. We can be productive and also waste time all in one day. I'm a social entrepreneur. There's never a shortage of things to do. And that doesn't need to stop me from choosing to use some of my time each day for other things and to build my own resilience. In fact, my work generally goes much better if I've been taking care of myself, and noticing, along the way as well.

Epilogue
Grow Your Garden

*"You never change things by fighting against
the existing reality.
To change something, build a new model that
makes the old one obsolete."*
- Buckminster Fuller

How to Start

At the end of all the decomposition and stirring and mixing your compost, you find yourself with a bucket full of good, nutritious soil. What then? Grow something! Plant something, then plant again. Some plants might thrive for you where you've planted them while others won't. Learn. Experiment. It's ok to start over. Amend the soil with more compost. Mix the soil properly for each plant and ensure the right amount of drainage.

Thepointistoalwayskeepgrowing-toactuallyliveyourlifewith intention and presence. Compost life's struggles into rich soil and use it to plant, tend, and grow your resilience practice and your life.

So now it's your turn. Maybe you are well along in your resilience journey. Maybe this is all new to you. Maybe you had a good thing going and now find yourself slipping. No problem. We can all begin again.

First, start small. Consistency wins over intensity. Resist the temptation to start by planning an entire life overhaul - yes, I know the allure and won't share the number of times I've tried it. And sure, you can plan long term. Still, start here and now with something small. Once you've got that going well, add something else that's small if you want. One day at a time, it will all come together.

Struggling to wrap your head around what you might do? I often find it useful to think about things in terms of start or restart, stop, and continue. What might you want to start doing? Perhaps you used to do something and don't anymore and you'd like to restart doing it again. What might you want to stop doing? What is holding you back right now and preventing you from building your resilience that you'd like to stop doing? What would you like to continue doing? What practices or perspectives do you already have that help you strengthen your resilience muscle?

Wondering what to try? Try everything until you find what works for you. Think about different ideas in terms of intention, mindfulness, reflection, creativity, nature, movement, connection, and community. How do you engage these elements in your life? How can you do so more effectively? Don't worry about not being good at something new you are thinking about trying. Learning new things is very good for our brains and mental health and we have to be prepared to be bad at them for a while. Remember that you do these things for the process, for you. The end product is not the focus of this experiment.

Now, think about change. How will you adapt as things change? You can keep this short-term to start. What are your options if something interrupts your planned schedule? How will you adjust as you experience shifting demands on your time and attention? What will you tell yourself if you miss doing something you had planned? How will you set yourself up for success to help you actually do what you've planned?

To establish new habits, we often need to do a couple things to set ourselves up for success. One is to eliminate even the smallest obstacles. If you're thinking about exercising first thing in the morning, for example, it helps to set out your exercise clothes. While it might seem silly, sometimes we use the silliest excuses to justify things to ourselves. At times, grabbing your exercise outfit from your closet seems like a step too far this morning. So eliminate that.

A second one is to think about what you will tell yourself when you start to fight yourself. Let's go back to the exercise example. You wake up, you see your clothes there, and you think: "I don't want to do this. I don't feel like it. I didn't sleep so well last night. I'm feeling a bit tired." You get the idea. We humans are quite adept at convincing ourselves of many things. So let's anticipate that. When your brain starts telling you no, how will you answer?

If my brain is telling me not to exercise, for example, I'll often say something like: "No, I'm just going to do it" or "It's ok, you'll feel better after" or "No thanks, let's go". I'll also think about the fact that there are no bad workouts, only ones you didn't do, and I may repeat that statement to myself a couple times. Sometimes I'll entice myself with a good playlist or my favorite color socks. It's the small things. Other times I'll approach it from a more existential perspective. I'll simply tell myself, I am doing this, because this is what I do now -

this is who I am.

If I really don't feel so great but am not actually sick, I'll do an easier workout remembering that consistency wins. For me, it's not important that I maximize every exercise session. I'm not training for anything. What's more important is that I do something, anything, every time, even if I have to drag myself metaphorically kicking and screaming for no good reason. Because those baby steps connect together to become something greater.

One of my favorite meme definitions of the word excuse is: a promise to ourselves that we will have the same issue again. I like to think about this and promise myself that, instead, I will intentionally make those choices as they come and take those baby steps - as many as I can manage.

So how about you? What will you start or restart, stop, and continue? How will you engage intention, reflection, creativity, nature, movement, connection, and community? How will you set yourself up for success? What small thing will you do right now, and again tomorrow, and also the next day?

And one more thing: don't be afraid of the difficulties in life and the garbage they bring with them. Get your composting system up and running and, with time and attention, transform the waste into nutritious soil in which to grow yourself. We may not want to experience difficulties in life, but we needn't fear them either. They are a natural part of a life of growth, transformation, and resilience.

Some Resources That Influenced My Thinking

Books
Essentialism: The Disciplined Pursuit of Less by Greg McKeown
Four Thousand Weeks: Time Management for Mortals by Oliver Burkeman
The Infinite Game by Simon Sinek
Think Again: The Power of Knowing What You Don't Know by Adam Grant

Songs
"How Do You Know" by Third Day
"Press On" by Billy Sprague

Videos, Talks, & People
John Paul Lederach talk at the 2018 On Being Gathering
Chimanande Adiche's Danger of a Single Story TED Talk
Linsey Pollack's Carrot Clarinet TED Talk
Nowness: Inside the Paris Opera Ballet video
Parker J. Palmer

Tools
PakDone
Owaves

Groups
Dancing Resilience Facebook Group
Evanston Folk Dancing

Acknowledgments

Many elements have finally come together to make this book possible. Among them, I must thank:

Pokhara, Nepal, and the many lake view cafes with endless supplies of various kinds of delicious momo and iced lemon mint. And of course the ever-present, majestic Annapurna mountains.

Good coffee, thanks to Kampong Coffee and my Minimex espresso machine, and my favorite coffee mug and easy chair, along with the myriad of sunrises that accompanied my regular writing time.

Owaves for helping me get my days together and so I could carve out that time in the first place.

Many people have also supported me throughout my journey - both in my pursuit of resilience and in writing this book. They are too many to name here, and among them I must thank:

Jeep Kanticha, who breathed the words to life in images.

Michael Wykoff, who helped refine it all and brought needed validation.

Lynn Howard, founder of LH Consulting, for always being generous with her time and knowledge and keeping me on track with the process.

Davina Liisa Pickering, founder of the Davina Liisa Method and practitioner of Five Elements Acupuncture, for helping me get my body working again and energy flowing properly.

All the people and groups I've worked with on resilience throughout the years.

My friends and colleagues from the Humanity's Thread community of practice who helped me hone my thoughts and approach: Charlie Allen, Emmanuel Habuka Bombande, Michael Fryer, John Paul Lederach, Chris Spies, Nomfundo Walaza, Herm Weaver.

My mentor, Emma Leslie, for the wisdom and pushes I needed along the way. I'll never forget that first conversation in your old office, and all the others since.

Brenda Sunoo and Jan Sunoo, long time friends who helped make this book so very much better than it was.

Mom and Dad for always believing in me more than I believe in myself.

About the Author

Jenn is a process facilitator and peacebuilder, building resilience into leadership development for the organizations and teams working to solve the world's most intractable problems. She is founder and CEO of Space Bangkok, a social enterprise that is based in Bangkok, Thailand, and works globally to support peacebuilding, resilience, leadership development, and strategic problem solving using creative facilitation, capacity building, and accompaniment.

Want to continue the conversation?
Find Jenn on LinkedIn at:
https://www.linkedin.com/in/jenn-weidman/.

www.ingramcontent.com/pod-product-compliance
Lightning Source LLC
Chambersburg PA
CBHW060327050426
42449CB00011B/2683